$38,000 For A Friendly Face

by

Kristin Shepherd

New York Hollywood London Toronto

SAMUELFRENCH.COM

Copyright © 2008 by Kristin Shepherd

ALL RIGHTS RESERVED

CAUTION: Professionals and amateurs are hereby warned that $38,000 FOR A FRIENDLY FACE is subject to a royalty. It is fully protected under the copyright laws of the United States of America, the British Commonwealth, including Canada, and all other countries of the Copyright Union. All rights, including professional, amateur, motion picture, recitation, lecturing, public reading, radio broadcasting, television and the rights of translation into foreign languages are strictly reserved. In its present form the play is dedicated to the reading public only.

The amateur live stage performance rights to $38,000 FOR A FRIENDLY FACE are controlled exclusively by Samuel French, Inc., and royalty arrangements and licenses must be secured well in advance of presentation. PLEASE NOTE that amateur royalty fees are set upon application in accordance with your producing circumstances. When applying for a royalty quotation and license please give us the number of performances intended, dates of production, your seating capacity and admission fee. Royalties are payable one week before the opening performance of the play to Samuel French, Inc., at 45 W. 25th Street, New York, NY 10010 or to Samuel French (Canada), Ltd., 100 Lombard Street, Lower Level, Toronto, Ontario, Canada M5C 1M3.

Royalty of the required amount must be paid whether the play is presented for charity or gain and whether or not admission is charged.

Stock royalty quoted upon application to Samuel French, Inc.

For all other rights than those stipulated above, apply to Samuel French, Inc., 45 West 25th Street, New York, NY 10010.

Particular emphasis is laid on the question of amateur or professional readings, permission and terms for which must be secured in writing from Samuel French, Inc.

Copying from this book in whole or in part is strictly forbidden by law, and the right of performance is not transferable.

Whenever the play is produced the following notice must appear on all programs, printing and advertising for the play: "Produced by special arrangement with Samuel French, Inc."

Due authorship credit must be given on all programs, printing and advertising for the play.

ISBN 978-0-573-65229-5   Printed in U.S.A.   #22313

No one shall commit or authorize any act or omission by which the copyright of, or the right to copyright, this play may be impaired.

No one shall make any changes in this play for the purpose of production.

Publication of this play does not imply availability for performance. Both amateurs and professionals considering a production are strongly advised in their own interests to apply to Samuel French, Inc., for written permission before starting rehearsals, advertising, or booking a theatre.

No part of this book may be reproduced, stored in a retrieval system, or transmitted in any form, by any means, now known or yet to be invented, including mechanical, electronic, photocopying, recording, videotaping, or otherwise, without the prior written permission of the publisher.

IMPORTANT BILLING AND CREDIT REQUIREMENTS

All producers of $38,000 FOR A FRIENDLY FACE *must* give credit to the Author of the Play in all programs distributed in connection with performances of the Play, and in all instances in which the title of the Play appears for the purposes of advertising, publicizing or otherwise exploiting the Play and/or a production. The name of the Author *must* appear on a separate line on which no other name appears, immediately following the title and *must* appear in size of type not less than fifty percent of the size of the title type.

$38,000 For A Friendly Face was first produced at The Nipissing University Theatre, North Bay, Ontario, in May, 2005. The production was produced by Claire Powers and under the direction of June Keevil with the following cast, crew and creative team:

ESTHER	Sally Macdonald
MARGE	Nancy Van der Schee
PYL (PHYLLIS) MCLEARY	Wendy Thoma
MATT	Bob Clout
JANE	Lorraine Conway
ANNIE	Kelly Maki
ALISON	Kim Bean
DELIVERIES FOR CARMICHAEL	Ashley Fricker
	Helen Monette
	Rick Lefebvre
ORGANIST	Cathy Coleman

Stage Manager: Vicky Boyer
Assistant Stage Manager: Emily Miller
Set Designer: Dennis Geden
Costume Design: Beth Jackson
Set Builder: Rob Ferron
Properties and Set Dressing: Nancy Davies
Lighting Design: Len Roy
Sound Design: Peter Nickle
Still Photography: Liz Lott
Scenic Painters: Nancy Davies, Claire Powers, Larry Lang
Makeup: Bunti Swanson
Hair: Jackie Larouche
Program/Graphic Design: Deb Sullivan
Front of House: Joyce Fell

CHARACTERS

MATT, new owner of the funeral home
JANE BAIN, daughter of the deceased
ESTHER, head of The Last Supper Committee
MARGE, member of The Last Supper Committee
PHYL (PHYLLIS MCLEARY), member of The Last Supper Committee
ALISON, flower deliverer
ANNIE BAIN, daughter of the deceased
VARIOUS DELIVERY PEOPLE (7), who may be played on stage or off

SETTING

The play takes place at the back of the funeral home, with the makeshift kitchen on one side and the chapel on the other. The bathroom is downstage of the kitchen and the back hallway is downstage of the chapel.

ACT ONE

Scene 1

(At the lectern, in the chapel. The delivery people can be played on stage or off)

(Enter **DELIVERY #1**)

MATT. *(who is earnest, eager to help, and not particularly confident)* Yes. Thanks. It goes in the front. If you turn right at the end of the hall, then it's, let's see, the first door on your left.

(Exit, **DELIVERY# 1**)

(Enter **DELIVERY #2**)

DELIVERY #2. Carmichael?

MATT. Hello. Yes, that goes in the front kitchen. If you go to the end of the hall, and turn left, it's the second door. *(Exit* **DELIVERY #2**) They're double. Double doors.

(Enter **DELIVERY #3**)

MATT. Are you with Carmichael or Bain?

DELIVERY #3. Carmichael.

MATT. These go in the front chapel. Just go to the end of this hall, and turn right. The first door on your left is the chapel. *(Exit* **DELIVERY #3**) It has an oak pedestal, about this high *(he indicates)*, just to the right of the door.

(Exit **DELIVERY #3**)

(Enter **DELIVERY #4**)

MATT. In the front, I think. If you follow her, you'll be all right.

(*Exit* **DELIVERY #4**)

(*Enter* **JANE**, *who is ill at ease and awkward*)

MATT. In the front, just down the hall, turn…. I'm sorry, what have you brought?

JANE. Nothing. Why?

MATT. You're here for Carmichael?

JANE. No. Bain.

(*Enter Delivery #5*)

DELIVERY #5. Carmichael.

MATT. (*to* **DELIVERY #5**) Oh. Just down the hall. Turn right at the end. Look for the….

(*Exit* **DELIVERY #5**)

JANE. I'm Jane. My mother is… (*she indicates "somewhere around here"*).

MATT. Of course, Miss Bain. We spoke last night. Come with me.

(*Exit* **MATT** *and* **JANE**)

Scene 2

(*In the kitchen*)

(*Enter* **ESTHER**, *dressed formally. Her hair has a ridiculously tight curl and she is wearing too much makeup. She puts a box of groceries on the counter and posts a menu for the day – sandwiches, squares, punch. She then exits to the bathroom to fix her hair and check her makeup.*)

(*Enter* **MARGE**, *whistling/humming. She reads the menu and stops whistling. She tears down the menu and then leaves.*)

(*Enter* **ESTHER**, *who begins unpacking the groceries.*)

(*Enter* **PHYL**, *dressed in black.*)

(*The women will unpack groceries and begin preparations during these scenes*)

PHYL: (*looking strangely at* **ESTHER**) Hi, Esther. Great hair.

ESTHER. Thank you.

PHYL. You know, there are boys out there on skateboards, practicing goodness-knows-what on those cement steps. They're going to kill themselves, not to mention their total lack of respect for the people trying to get inside. Imagine trying to dodge sharp, flying *weapons*, really, aren't they, when your heart is bursting with grief. Bursting.

ESTHER. I've got ham, tuna, and egg, on white and brown – well, 60% whole wheat. I worked like a demon last night. Marge is bringing her date squares and the pineapple-carrot Jello.

PHYL. Those squares are fabulous. So small, so perfect for the mourners. Nothing so big you'd choke on it.

ESTHER. I told her to start cutting them smaller. They go further that way. No one'll take three. They'll take two, no matter how big, but they feel like pigs taking three.

PHYL. Pigs, Esther? These people have lost loved ones.

ESTHER. Well, they haven't lost their appetites, have they? And we do have a budget to keep in mind.

PHYL. Are you all right today, Esther? You're not getting that chest cold, are you?

ESTHER. No, I feel fine.

PHYL. So did Susan's mother, and then, wham, it was pneumonia, and you know what happened then.

ESTHER: I feel fine, Phyl. Do I not look fine?

PHYL. You look very colourful. (*She pauses, seeing* **ESTHER**'s *reaction.*) Like spring, I suppose.

ESTHER. Good. That's what I was aiming for.

PHYL. It's October.

ESTHER. I know.

PHYL. You never wear makeup.

ESTHER. I know. I just thought, it's fall, and a bit of makeup makes sense in the fall, when you're paler. As a rule.

PHYL. Well, as long as you're all right.

(*Enter* **MARGE**, *with grocery bags.*)

MARGE. Gorgeous day out there. What's with the hair, Esther?

PHYL. Hi Marge. It's a spring look she's aiming at.

MARGE. Well, it's…stunning. And your makeup is…stunning.

ESTHER. Thank you.

MARGE. (*with an edge*) And Phyl, my friend, you look radiant again today.

PHYL. Don't start, Marge.

MARGE. Colour is good, Phyl.

PHYL. It doesn't seem fair to the deceased.

ESTHER. The deceased don't care.

PHYL. Or to the loved ones. Imagine that burden of loss. The heaviness. The sheer….

MARGE. We don't have to harp on it.

PHYL: Would you rather we were tap dancing, Marge? Or skateboarding down cement steps with no helmets on? Last Supper Committee. That's the name.

MARGE. God, they look fantastic out there. Don't you wish you could try it?

PHYL. No, I don't, and I'm not sure what God has to do with it one way or another.

ESTHER. Well, there are only three of us this morning, hardly enough to call us a committee. We'll have to work like fiends to get enough ready.

PHYL. Things'll be different back here. No dishwasher, no ovens, no sinks. How'll we do this without a sink?

ESTHER. We'll just do it, that's how. Carmichael is at four in the main chapel. It's being catered in the kitchen.

PHYL. Catered? That sounds fancy.

ESTHER: Beef stew, mashed potatoes, mixed vegetables – good luck keeping *those* from drying out for 180 people. Anyway, Matt asked if I'd do the Bain food back here. We have a sink in the bathroom. We have cutlery that doesn't match. It'll be a smaller event. Nothing wrong with sandwiches and squares.

MARGE. Who's doing the Carmichael food?

ESTHER. Helen.

MARGE/PHYL. Oh/Ah.

ESTHER. He needed a caterer. It's just business.

PHYL/MARGE. Just business/Of course/That's right/Absolutely/Oh yeah.

ESTHER. I am completely organized.

PHYL. Is it a 2pm funeral?

ESTHER. 2pm, but not a funeral. Just a visitation, so we'll need the food for 2. And we don't know the numbers, so I'm prepared for 40. We'll make do if more show up.

PHYL. 2pm is the best time. Gives you a chance to wake up, get your feet under you, but not so late in the day that you're too tired for your grief.

ESTHER/MARGE. Mmm.

PHYL. And a visitation is a good choice. Of course, some need the full funeral, the reality of the casket, and that walk down the aisle,....

MARGE. Phyl....

ESTHER. I should say something about the casket for this one.

(*Enter* **ALISON**, *while* **ESTHER** *is speaking.* **ALISON** *is surly by nature.*)

PHYL. What? What is it?

ALISON. Flowers. (*No one hears her.*)

ESTHER. It's just that....

PHYL. Is it oak? I love oak. Oak is so dignified. Even if it's just veneer.

MARGE. Phyl, for God's sake.

PHYL. What? And do you really need to take the Lord's name in vain, here?

Is it not oak, then?

ESTHER. No, it isn't oak. That isn't it.

PHYL. Is it maple? It wouldn't be mahogany.

MARGE. Don't encourage her, Esther.

ESTHER. Forget the casket, then.

PHYL. We'll see it soon enough, I suppose.

MARGE. We'll all see it soon enough.

ESTHER. I made up the menu.

PHYL. Where? (*The board is blank.*)

ESTHER. Marge, that's you, isn't it?

MARGE. I'm going to die if I have to eat crustless sandwiches one more time.

ESTHER. Crusts are too messy.

PHYL. You'd hardly want to choke on crusts while you're saying your final goodbyes.

ESTHER. Crumbs all over the place.

MARGE. I like the crusts.

PHYL. Needing the Heimlich manoeuvre when you're so inconsolable that you're doubled over already.

ESTHER. I'd spend my entire life vacuuming.

MARGE. I like the crusts.

ALISON. Flowers.

ESTHER/PHYL/MARGE. What?

ALISON. Flower delivery. For Bain.

ESTHER. Mrs. Bain is no longer with us, thank you very much, but you can bring them in here. You're two hours late.

ALISON. Whatever.

(*Exit* **ALISON**)

ESTHER. She's a treat.

PHYL. She looks a little pale.

MARGE. I thought a salmon soufflé.

ESTHER. Well that's daft.

PHYL. You know, Marge, last time you wanted a lobster mousse, and the time before last, for Susan's funeral, you wanted something else....

ESTHER. It was asparagus and goat cheese frittatas, for 64 guests. And even if you could do warm frittatas for 64, which you cannot, asparagus and goat cheese, Marge? What were you thinking? Even if it tasted good, and that's hard to imagine, we'd be stuck with festering leftovers, and we have exactly no money for that.

MARGE. (*firmly*) I thought a salmon soufflé.

ESTHER. Marge, you have date squares.

MARGE. No, actually, I don't.

ESTHER. It says on my list that you have date squares and your Jello mould.

MARGE. No mould.

ESTHER. Carrot-pineapple. Look. It's number three on my list.

PHYL. Your squares are so perfect, Marge. They're so small.

ESTHER. Organization, Marge. I don't know what you're doing with this salmon thing....

MARGE. Susan loved asparagus, that's all, and I like salmon.

PHYL. Susan was such a wonderful cook.

MARGE. She was a terrible cook.

PHYL. What a thing to say!

ESTHER. If we don't get a grip on things here, Matt'll never make it.

MARGE. You're very devoted for a volunteer.

PHYL. Not to mention that other thing.

ESTHER. Thank you so much for not mentioning that other thing, Phyl. I am devoted to no one. I just hate to see

him bungle this before he even gets it off the ground.
PHYL. If you say so.
ESTHER. I say so. Listen, I don't want to be picky about this, but we can't afford your soufflé, Marge.
MARGE. I made it last night. With my own ingredients. No charge.
ESTHER. (*offended*) I see. Well. I suppose we can make room on the menu. As long as nothing else changes. There's no time to make Jello, now, of course, so that's a change of plans, but I may be able to find some date squares downtown. If I get a minute.
PHYL. Sheila dropped off a vegetable tray this morning. I have it with me.
ESTHER. Good, that's good. With her dip?
PHYL. Two cups of ranch. I love that dip.
ESTHER. Two cups, that'll be tight.
MARGE. I also brought jalapeno pie.
ESTHER. Jalapeno pie? That sounds hot!
MARGE. It's October. Hot is good.
ESTHER. You know, Marge, I have four-and-a-half scrapbooks of inexpensive and delicious snack foods to choose from. There's no reason to go out of your way to burn their tongues off.
MARGE. Come on, Esther! Are you not completely sick of Ordinary Funerals?
ESTHER. What? Would you prefer Salmon Funerals? A Jalapeno Funeral?
MARGE. Yes I would, as a matter of fact.
ESTHER. This is completely ridiculous! And Matt is counting on me to…. Phyl? Help me out, here.
PHYL. Well, people do need comforting food when they're grieving, Marge. I don't know how comforting the jalapeno would be in a dark time.
ESTHER. Jesus Murphy, a dark time. Listen, Marge. If this costs us a penny….
MARGE. Not a penny.

PHYL. And who is Jesus Murphy, I'd like to know.

ESTHER. Or if people laugh, or they're offended....

MARGE. They won't be. They'll be thrilled to see something other than egg salad and tuna.

ESTHER. Well my sandwiches are already made. Egg salad *and* tuna *and* ham. I spent hours on them last night, and I'm taking the crusts off. No discussion.

MARGE. So we'll do both.

ESTHER. I will not let this be a disaster.

MARGE. My soufflé'll bring the house down.

PHYL. I don't know. It sounds airy. Light.

ESTHER. I can just imagine Helen....

PHYL. A bit flaky, almost.

MARGE. Helen'll be envious. There's no way she could do soufflés for 180.

ESTHER. I'll have to reorganize everything. I want the sandwiches and squares up front.

MARGE. OK.

ESTHER. I'm flexible.

MARGE. You're going to hurt yourself, you're so flexible.

PHYL. Do you remember Fran's last summer? Her husband brought in those mincemeat pies.

ESTHER. No one ate them.

PHYL. Mincemeat is more a Christmas thing. He didn't know any better. The grief! The agony!

ESTHER. I may be too flexible.

MARGE. I don't think so.

ESTHER. I go with the flow.

MARGE. You certainly do.

(*Enter* **ALISON**)

ALISON. Flowers.

MARGE. What's your name?

ALISON. Alison.

MARGE. What's your favourite food, Alison?

ESTHER. What are you doing, Marge? Why does that matter?

ALISON. I don't like food.

ESTHER. Good.

MARGE. Well, if you did like food, what would you like?

ESTHER. Marge.

ALISON. Breakfast, maybe.

ESTHER. Marge, it's a funeral.

MARGE. It isn't a funeral, it's a visitation. What kind of breakfast?

ESTHER: I'll take the flowers. You can think about breakfast while you bring in the rest. It might be faster if you bring in more than three at a time.

ALISON. There are no more.

ESTHER. What?

ALISON: This is it.

ESTHER. We have three flowers for the funeral?

PHYL. Thank goodness it's *not* a funeral.

ESTHER. Thundering mother of God. Three flowers?

PHYL. Thundering what, Esther?

ESTHER. I ordered three dozen. Did you make this mistake?

MARGE. Esther, I saw buckets of flowers on the way in.

ESTHER. Those are for Carmichael. There isn't one arrangement for Bain yet. Not one.

PHYL. Oh, no. That isn't good.

MARGE. It's early. There'll be flowers.

ALISON. Cream of wheat, maybe.

ESTHER. Mother of God, I don't believe it.

MARGE. Do you spice it up at all?

PHYL. That's Mary, Esther, and yes, she *is* the mother of God.

ALISON. Why?

MARGE. We're trying something new.

ALISON. My brother used to put those stupid cinnamon hearts in mine.

ESTHER. That is absurd.

MARGE. I like it.

PHYL. This is going to be some funeral.

MARGE. It's not a funeral.

ESTHER. Jesus Murphy.

PHYL. Esther.

ESTHER. Jesus Murphy.

ALISON. Whatever.

Scene 3

(*In the chapel, which has seen better days*)

(**MATT** *ushers* **JANE** *into the chapel. During the scene he rearranges the empty vases in an attempt to make the file boxes look more elegant/funereal.*)

MATT. Here we are, Miss Bain.

JANE. (*trying, at first, to find out how much Matt knows about her mother*) Thank you for taking care of things. My mother was…. Well, you probably knew her.

MATT. No, I didn't, really.

JANE. Well, she was…. It's important to me that her funeral is as…because she was so….

MATT. Of course it will be. Although you understand there won't be an actual funeral for your mother.

JANE. Yes, yes, you said that.

MATT. She may have discussed it with you.

JANE. We didn't…actually…get around to that.

MATT. Some people don't like to burden their children.

(**JANE** *stares at him.*)

MATT: She chose a very simple event, really, and she didn't specify much about the details. Probably leaving that up to us to discuss together.

JANE. All right, then. I'm ready.

MATT. These events really are more for the living than the not-living. The beyond-living. Unless, of course, we consider the question of an afterlife, in which case she's still…alive, but in a different…living…arrangement.

JANE. Oh God!

MATT. What?

JANE. Still alive? Jesus.

MATT. No, no. Don't even…. I was on the wrong…. Let's talk about our Celebration of Life. We'll put your pictures up – you brought pictures?

JANE. A couple, but I don't think…they aren't exactly….

MATT: Good, and perhaps, later, we'll discuss some stories, ones you'd like to share with friends at the Celebration.

JANE. (*horrified*) Friends?

MATT. When will your family be joining us?

JANE. Our family is…very, very small.

MATT. How small?

JANE. Extremely small.

MATT. I see.

JANE. You know, this place is so dark, it's a bit claustrophobic. I wonder if we could go …. I mean, at some point…. My mother…. I really need to see that she's…permanently…settled in here. (*quietly*) Dead.

MATT. Oh. Well of course she is.

JANE. So she's here somewhere.

MATT. She's right here. This is our Sunshine Chapel. This is where we'll be celebrating this afternoon.

(JANE *says nothing. She is not comforted by this room.*)

MATT. The Sunshine Chapel is perfectly suited, I think, to an intimate event.

JANE: Intimate?

MATT. Intimate. Less…impersonal. More…personal. Of course, if we need more room for the guests we can open that wall up into the hall. It's a retractable wall. It's new.

JANE. So she'll be in here?

MATT. She is here. Right over there. (**MATT** *points to two small boxes*)

JANE. Where?

MATT. Right there.

JANE. By the boxes?

MATT. That's her casket. (*He sees* **JANE**'s *reaction.*) Maybe I should open up that wall right now.

JANE. Those are file boxes.

MATT. It was her casket of choice, Miss Bain. She wanted something simple, something understated, something less ornate.

JANE. My mother is in there?

MATT. Yes, she is. She said the smaller interim resting place would suit her more than adequately.

JANE. There are two boxes.

MATT. Pardon?

JANE. Why are there two boxes?

MATT. I thought we might get to that. Tough to avoid it, really.

JANE. Where is my mother, exactly? Which one is she in?

MATT. It's a delicate situation. She's…she's in both.

JANE. She's in both boxes?

MATT. Both *caskets*, yes.

JANE. I don't understand.

MATT. Actually, for the most part, she's in the one on the left.

JANE. Jesus!

MATT. The smaller one.

JANE. Jesus.

MATT. It's just her hip in the other one.

JANE. I'm going to throw up.

MATT. Her right hip. The titanium. It doesn't cremate. She wanted a separate casket for it. A kind of co-casket. A matching casket.

JANE. Matching caskets?

MATT. Would you like some time with her?

JANE. To do what?

MATT. Well, I thought….

JANE. Do you mean alone with her? With the boxes?

MATT. The caskets, yes. You said you wanted to see that she was…. permanently…settled in.

JANE. (*urgently looking for an exit*) I don't think so.

MATT. I'm sorry. Is there no one we can call for you?

JANE. No. I'm fine.

MATT. Anyone.

JANE. There is no one.

ANNIE. (*from off stage*) Janie?

MATT. Who's that?

ANNIE. Janie?

MATT. There's someone calling your name.

JANE. There is not.

(*Enter* **ANNIE**, *with a takeout coffee cup*)

ANNIE. Janie! Hey, bit of a miracle finding you back here. There's some kind of huge party being set up out front.

MATT. Hello.

ANNIE. Hello back.

(**ANNIE** *places her coffee cup on one of the coffins.* **MATT** *picks it up.*)

MATT. I'm Matt Watson, funeral director here.

ANNIE. Annie Bain.

MATT. Jane's…?

JANE. No relation. / **ANNIE.** Sister.

MATT. (*not understanding*) Oh, I see. All right, then. Why don't I check on the flowers? They're late.

JANE. I hate flowers.

ANNIE. Bit gloomy back here. 'Course it suits the occasion. Not to mention the star of the occasion. Do you have an ashtray?

MATT. No, actually, there's no smoking in the building. Why don't I….

ANNIE. (*interrupting*) It's a bit late for the second hand to be hurting anyone in here, don't you think? (**JANE** *grabs her arm*) Ow!

JANE. Stop it.

MATT. Good, then. Right.

(*Exit* **MATT**)

ANNIE. Let go of my cigarettes. Hey, it's good to see you. I'm not staying.

JANE. You're what?

ANNIE. Not staying.

JANE. But you're here.

ANNIE. Passing through.

JANE. You're four hours from home.

ANNIE. I needed some milk. What time's the funeral?

JANE. She didn't want a funeral. It's a visitation. A gathering of friends.

ANNIE. (*incredulously*) Friends?

JANE. I know. You're not staying?

ANNIE. Nope.

JANE. You drove four hours to say hello?

ANNIE. I needed 2%.

JANE. 2%.

ANNIE. For the cottage.

JANE. What cottage?

ANNIE. Peter's cottage.

JANE. Who's Peter?

ANNIE. Just a guy.

JANE. You're missing this…for a guy?

ANNIE. I'll be heartbroken to miss the whole visitation thing, but yeah.

JANE. Is he important, this guy?

ANNIE. Don't know. I'll let you know if it turns into something.

JANE. How old is he?

ANNIE. He's 62 or –3, I guess.

JANE. A toddler.

ANNIE. You're still so quick to say the shittiest thing you can think of.

JANE. Well, what can I say? I'm happy for you. Again.

ANNIE. Anyway, she said, to change the subject, I need the milk, and there's a Mac's on the main drag. They have good 2% there. Hey. Where *is* the belle of the ball? The witch of the west.

JANE. Keep your voice down.

ANNIE. Is she freshening up somewhere?

JANE. She's over there.

ANNIE. Where?

JANE. There.

ANNIE. By the file boxes?

JANE. Sort of.

ANNIE. What do you mean, sort of?

JANE. She's inside. I hope she's inside.

ANNIE. She's smaller than I remember. But that's the thing about gravity, right? You just keep shrinking.

JANE. Except there are two of her, now.

ANNIE. How long's it been since you've heard from her? (**JANE** *doesn't answer*) Not long enough, I guess. You know, if gravity still works after you're dead, they'll be to move her to a pizza box soon.

JANE. God, I hope she's in there.

ANNIE. Then we'll read about it at the check-out at Loblaws.

Unpleasant Dead Woman Found in Manilla Envelope.

JANE. It's a casket.

ANNIE. A manilla casket.

JANE. It's her interim resting place.

ANNIE. Manilla interim resting place.

JANE. You're such an ass.

ANNIE. And you're a fart sniffer. What's in the other box? Did she take a friend with her?

JANE. No. It's all her.

ANNIE. In both boxes?

JANE. Yeah.

ANNIE. What a freak.

JANE. Why could she not pick one box? Then you'd know she was dead, wouldn't you, you'd know she was all in one place and done with.

ANNIE. Half for you, half for…whoever else wants her. Maybe half of her'll be easier to live with. Especially dead.

JANE. It isn't half. She's mostly in the one on the left. It's her hip in the one on the right.

ANNIE. Holy shit. (*She begins to laugh*).

JANE. It's titanium. Leave it to her to start multiplying just when she's supposed to go away for good.

ANNIE. (*with false sincerity*) You seem bothered by it, Janie.

JANE. What I'm bothered by is you, Annie. (*pause*) I didn't mean that. So, did you take the weekend off?

ANNIE. I took the foreseeable future off.

JANE. You mean you quit?

ANNIE. Yeah.

JANE. Again.

ANNIE. Yeah.

JANE. Well, why change, right?

ANNIE. It was Crappy Tire. Don't get your holier-than-thou going. Besides, I have other possibilities.

JANE: (*sarcastically*) Yeah? What kind of possibilities?

ANNIE. It's nothing. Forget it. Right, Mom?

JANE. Quiet.

ANNIE. Jane, Jane, Jane. I don't think you can hear much once you're in the ashtray.

JANE. Jesus, Annie. Stop talking like that.

ANNIE. What? It is basically an ashtray, isn't it? Or two ashtrays.

JANE. You're such a jerk. (*Pause, and she indicates that she didn't mean that, either*) Of course, there'll be no one here.

ANNIE. I know.

JANE. You should stay.

ANNIE. I'll stay for coffee if you'd like, despite the fact that you don't seem to have changed since forever. We can do root canals on each other, stick forks in each others' eyes if you'd like. But I am not staying for any fond farewell with the cardboard boxes. I need milk. Excuse me.

(*Exit* **ANNIE**)

Scene 4

(*In the kitchen*)

ALISON. You can't make me stay.

ESTHER. No I can't. But I can call Rose's Roses and ask who was responsible for bringing three flowers.

ALISON. Go ahead and call them. See if I care.

ESTHER. You could be fired for a thing like that. A funeral with three flowers.

ALISON. I said go ahead and call. You'd be doing me a favour.

PHYL. Do you remember what Rose did for Gillian's, that huge wreath, all yellow roses.

MARGE. She had lousy taste in men, that Gillian.

PHYL. I don't think there was a dry eye in front of that wreath.

ALISON. Most people think that three dozen roses stuffed in a wire form means you're gifted.

ESTHER: She'll be sold out for Carmichael by now. My God, I won't be able to find dandelions for these people.

PHYL. My gosh.

ALISON. It's a stupid place to work. I was going to quit anyway.

PHYL. Quit and do what?

ALISON. Maybe start my own place.

ESTHER. You've certainly got the personality for it.

ALISON. You know, this is also a stupid place.

MARGE. No it isn't. Esther's a little tense today, that's all.

PHYL. A little dressed up. She might have a fever.

ESTHER. I do not have a fever. And what do you mean by a little dressed up?

PHYL. Do you want me to feel your forehead, Esther?

ESTHER. No, Phyl, I do not. For God's sake.

PHYL. No need to drag God into this.

MARGE. Why don't you help us out, Alison? We're short, today, and I could use your help with the cilantro.

ESTHER. Cilantro?!

MARGE. It's a garnish, Esther, it's nothing. (*to* **ALISON**) And you can tell us all about quitting, and cream of wheat, with the hearts. What do you say?

ESTHER. Marge, we are not doing porridge.

MARGE. Are you from around here, Alison?

ALISON. Mason.

MARGE. But you live here, now?

ALISON. I do.

PHYL. Married?

(**ALISON** *doesn't respond.*)

MARGE. No need to tell us everything right off the bat.

Here, scissors are better for that. (*As soon as* **ALISON** *finishes cutting the cilantro, she'll begin cutting flowers out of the paper in which she brought the flowers, and whatever paper she can find after that. Her cutting will go on through most of Act One.*)

ESTHER. Three flowers.

MARGE. Esther, people will bring more.

ESTHER. But the daughter'll be here by now. It'll look like nobody loves anyone in there.

MARGE. Esther?

ESTHER. Yes, Marge.

MARGE. Leave it alone, all right?

ESTHER. Leave it alone, she says.

PHYL. I love these little sandwiches.

MARGE. Who was she, Mrs. Bain? Was she that short woman with the little dog on Main West?

PHYL. It's a Cairn terrier, that dog. I think it's diabetic.

ESTHER. No, that's Nora Stewart. She moved into town with her dog after her husband…. You know. What an idiot.

PHYL. He was a good man!

MARGE. Phyl, he set fire to your brother's barn. He was crazy.

ESTHER. He was a little off, Phyl. Mrs. Bain lived on Ferguson, right by the piano teacher's place.

MARGE. Which house?

ESTHER. You know that little bungalow with the yellow carport?

PHYL. Why a carport on that corner and not a garage, I don't know. Pretty risky.

ESTHER. Exactly. The north wind'll bury a car in there, but she was a Southerner. Must not have known any better.

MARGE. Southerner from where?

ESTHER. The City.

MARGE/PHYL. Ahhh/Ohh.

MARGE. How old was she?

ESTHER. Mid-sixties, maybe. There's a daughter from out of town.

PHYL. Her husband?

ESTHER. Matt says no husband.

PHYL. Poor thing. Church?

ESTHER. None.

PHYL. Southerner. No church. No husband.

MARGE. (*sarcastically*) How *did* she survive?

ESTHER. Never at bingo. I'd have seen her at the door.

PHYL. Legion?

ESTHER. No. What about the pool?

MARGE. I never saw her.

PHYL. How can nobody know her? How long did she live here?

ESTHER. Ten years anyway, Matt said.

PHYL. She couldn't have spent all that time alone.

ESTHER. She came through the store often enough. She wasn't nice. Cold, standoffish. Some people have a way.

PHYL. Were you friendly back?

ESTHER. Not especially.

ALISON. Surprise.

ESTHER. It's hard to be friendly to rude people. (*to* **ALISON**) Here. Cut this tag off for me. Please.

PHYL. What did she buy?

ESTHER. She liked that trail mix, the kind with the dried cranberries. That's the most expensive mix in stock, except at Christmas. And Earl Grey tea. And imported shortbread. Who'd buy cookies that have been around long enough to be shipped from overseas, I don't know, and pay through the teeth for them.

PHYL. Imported shortbread.

ESTHER. I'm not on cash very often, I don't remember

what else.

PHYL. How did she die?

ESTHER. I don't know.

PHYL. Someone must know.

ESTHER. Matt'll know. He's not saying.

PHYL. Maybe it was an aneurysm.

ESTHER. Matt didn't say.

PHYL. Barb's aunt had an aneurysm. Happened like that, she smacked her head against the shower wall, broke five tiles – smashed them to pieces the size of loonies – and never made it out of the tub.

ALISON. Gross.

MARGE. Phyl, does it ever occur to you that you might be kind of obsessed with all of this?

ESTHER. Marge.

PHYL. I don't know what you're talking about. I am not obsessed. Who made her funeral arrangements?

ESTHER. She did. Last winter.

PHYL. Some people know their time is near. It gives them time to prepare for the end. That's lucky.

MARGE. Like winning the 6/49.

ESTHER. Mrs. Bain was perfect that way. Came in early, made her choices. Paid in full.

PHYL. Paid in full?

ESTHER. Now that's lucky. Phyl, is that it for the squares?

PHYL. Paid in full? I thought she didn't have much money.

ESTHER. That cranberry trail mix? She had money. I'll have to cut them in half again. We'll spread them out.

PHYL. You know, I do know one little thing about the deceased.

ESTHER. What's that?

PHYL. From the library. I suppose confidentiality doesn't matter so much now that she's gone to her peaceful resting ground. Well, and now that I'm leaving.

MARGE. Not yet, you're not.

PHYL. Actually I am.

MARGE. You have a year left.

PHYL. No.

MARGE. Phyl? What are you talking about?

PHYL. It's nothing.

ESTHER. What about Mrs. Bain?

PHYL. Bronwyn, her name was. Bronwyn Bain!

ESTHER. I thought you didn't know her.

MARGE. You never mentioned knowing her.

PHYL. She was a patron at the library. And we had a kind of…well, a kind of relationship, I suppose. Not a friendship, really, but a…an understanding. Perhaps.

ESTHER. What the heck does that mean? An understanding?

MARGE. A relationship of some kind?

ESTHER. Perhaps?

PHYL. She didn't give a hoot about what anyone thought. As though she didn't need another soul in this world.

ESTHER. As though she was better than the rest of us.

PHYL. Maybe. That's what the others thought. But she was so fierce about it. I'd like to be fierce.

MARGE. What was this understanding?

ESTHER. This relationship of some kind?

ALISON. Perhaps.

ESTHER. (*snapping*) Alison, we can't get a word in edgewise.

ALISON: Excuse me for breathing.

MARGE. Honey, she's joking. Aren't you, Esther?

ESTHER. Yes, I'm joking. What relationship?

PHYL. Mrs. Bain – Bronwyn – died with $377 outstanding in overdue fines.

ESTHER. $377? How many books did she take out?

PHYL. Only two at a time. It was more the number of times she took books out. Two books each time. Thirty-four times. Sixty-eight books in total.

MARGE. You can't do that. Ray tries to do that, 'cause he can't be bothered to look under the bed for his old books, but they won't give him any new ones till he brings them back. It's the only exercise he gets, reaching under the bed.

ESTHER. And Matt! I find his books lying all over the place here. He'd owe millions if it weren't for me. I know the rules. You have to pay, or no more books.

PHYL. And there was our relationship, I guess. She'd come in without her books, and bring two new ones to the counter. Always to me, as far as I know. I'd explain the overdue policy and she'd thank me, with this grim mouth and one eyebrow hiked way up. I can't even do that thing with one eyebrow. And I just did it. Checked two more out.

ALISON. I'll bet you can catch a bit of hell for that.

PHYL. Yes, you can.

ESTHER. She probably had a nice little library at home by the end.

MARGE. What kind of trouble did they give you, Phyl?

PHYL. They called it an unexpected disappointment, an unfortunate ending to a career. They moved my retirement date up.

ALISON. They canned you?

PHYL. No, they didn't fire me, exactly.

MARGE. When are you finished?

PHYL. Yesterday. At three.

MARGE. Oh, Phyl.

ESTHER. Phyl.

PHYL: You know, I went on checking out books to Mrs. Bain, even after I'd been reprimanded. Seven more times. Fourteen books.

ALISON. That is great.

ESTHER. What?

PHYL. Do you think so?

ESTHER. What that is is complete disregard for your own rules.

MARGE. Oh, Phyl.

ESTHER: I smell onions. It's not right to have onions at a funeral.

MARGE. It isn't a funeral. Don't worry about it, Esther.

ESTHER. Don't worry about it, she says.

MARGE. Jalapenos and onions. They're fantastic for you.

PHYL. I wonder what a woman like that would choose for her own funeral service?

ESTHER. I'm going to say one more thing about Mrs. Bain.

MARGE. My God, did everyone know her?

PHYL. What about her?

ESTHER. I'm just going to say it and then we'll leave it, I don't want to discuss it at all. And I don't want any strange looks in front of the family or friends.

PHYL. It's open casket, isn't it? I love open casket.

ALISON. That's morbid.

PHYL. I'll be here for this one.

ESTHER. You're here for every one.

MARGE. I may stay for this one, too.

ESTHER/PHYL. What?

MARGE. Is there something wrong with that?

ESTHER. No.

PHYL. No.

ESTHER. I might as well tell you, then. It isn't open casket.

MARGE. Good.

PHYL. That's a shame. Rachel had open casket. She looked fantastic, except, you know, I never saw Rachel's mouth closed while she was alive – you know how she loved to talk – so it was a little unnatural, I thought, seeing her in that casket, with her lips pressed together.

ESTHER. Well, there's no more mouth for Mrs. Bain, open or closed.

MARGE. God almighty.

ALISON. Shit.

PHYL. There's no need…. No more mouth? What do you mean, no more mouth?

ESTHER. She was cremated.

PHYL. Before the service? Susan did that, too. They put her in that gorgeous red dress of hers, that washable silk she bought for their thirtieth – do you remember it, Esther? She looked so happy in it – and then they cremated her, dress and all.

MARGE. Don't start, Phyl.

PHYL. Red pumps and all.

MARGE. Here we go.

PHYL. Mouth and all.

ALISON. Gross.

ESTHER. Here's the thing. She's in two boxes.

PHYL/MARGE. What?

ESTHER. Mrs. Bain. She's in two little caskets.

PHYL. Two caskets?

ALISON. Holy shit.

MARGE. It's about time.

PHYL. What do you mean, about time?

ESTHER. Not a word more, now. We're done with it.

ALISON. Maybe one is full of books.

ESTHER. We will not discuss it. Let's get to work.

PHYL. I hope *they* weren't cremated. That'd be illegal, burning library books.

Two boxes? I've never heard of that.

ESTHER. Let's just leave it alone.

PHYL. Was she a huge woman?

MARGE. This is good.

ESTHER. I said no discussion.

PHYL. Maybe some people just turn into more ash than others. My Uncle Lanny needed an extra large urn. He was a gem of a man, but he was dense.

ESTHER. Enough! God almighty.

PHYL. No need toss the Almighty around, Esther. Two caskets!

(*This conversation fades out*)

Scene 5

(*In the chapel.* **JANE** *is sorting through pictures.*)

(*Enter* **MATT**, *with a lamp and a purse. From time to time, he shifts the two caskets in an attempt to make them look like one entity.*)

MATT. Excuse me, Miss Bain. I thought I'd just add a little light. So it won't feel so claustrophobic. So gloomy. Because this should really be a happy occasion. (**JANE** *does not look happy.*) Well, a time of contemplation and reflection, certainly, but with some…happy…(*He plugs in the lamp, turns it on.*) under…tones. How are the pictures coming?

JANE. They're fine.

MATT. Why don't we have a look together?

JANE. No.

MATT. I can do that, if you like.

JANE. No, they're no good, they're…overexposed. Besides, there'll be nobody…. I like your purse.

MATT. Actually, it isn't mine.

JANE. It's a great colour on you.

MATT. It's your mother's.

JANE. No, I don't think so.

MATT. It is. I thought you might…

JANE. All right, all right, that's enough. Maybe it is hers.

MATT. It is. She asked me to find it at her house after her… passing.

JANE: Did she say anything…

MATT. Anything….?

JANE. Anything, oh, I don't know, at all, about anything.

MATT. She said she'd leave the final financial arrangements. For today's…events here.

JANE. Oh, okay.

MATT. But that's not…. I thought you might *like* something personal. There are a few things inside.

JANE. (*staring, horrified, at the purse*) Sure. That's just great.

MATT. I have some thoughts on your mother's Celebration.

JANE. Oh.

MATT. I mentioned earlier that we might have family and friends share stories. Memories, if you will, of your mother's life. They say that sharing helps everyone in times of grief.

JANE. Do they say that?

MATT. If we can get your stories first, I'll be able to write a warmer, and perhaps a more meaningful obituary for this afternoon's guests.

JANE. Guests?

MATT. If you're uncomfortable, speaking in front of people, you could both share a few stories with me, and I could relate them to the others. Whatever makes you comfortable.

JANE. Mr....

MATT. Watson. They say that sharing grief helps to ....

JANE. My sister's gone. To get milk. 2%. She might not be back.

MATT. She'll be back in time for the visitation.

JANE. No....

MATT. She can share then if she'd like. Or not. There's no pressure around this.

JANE. Well, it's interesting that you say that, because it feels like an awful lot of pressure. Here. (*She hands him the pictures.*)

MATT. You know, I think these will be just.... (*He looks through the pictures, holding them up. The father's head is cut out of each picture.*) Well, isn't that something.

JANE. The holes are my dad. My mother was very good with scissors.

MATT. Remarkable.

JANE. She was extremely crafty.

MATT. What I meant was....

JANE. She could cut just about anything. With scissors, with an exacto knife. Steak knife, potato peeler, she could really cut.

MATT. They say time is a great healer.

JANE. Who says that?

MATT. What?

JANE. Who says that about time?

MATT. (*pause*) They do.

JANE. (*angrily*) Well that's really good to know, isn't it, because they must know what they're talking about. I'm sorry. It was nice outside this morning.

MATT. October is a good month.

JANE. Yeah.

MATT. The colours.

JANE. Yeah.

MATT. There are fewer crimes committed in October, on average.

JANE. Crimes?

MATT. Yes, I think people are just happier in the cooler weather. Even the criminals.

JANE. Are you worried I'm a criminal?

MATT. No!

JANE. Well, who are the criminals?

MATT. I'm sorry, I've got that wrong. Wrong direction altogether.

JANE. I can't figure out what's happening here. With all of this. I don't know what to do.

MATT. Well, let's look for one good thing, one comforting thing, for instance, something....

JANE. Comforting? You know, if I wanted comfort, I'd go home.

MATT. I suppose so.

JANE. I mean, what's comfortable about this? Would you be here if you were looking for comfort?

MATT. I.... I haven't thought about that. Maybe I haven't

got that right, that part.

JANE. I think my mother might stay put, but wouldn't the rest of us just go home?

MATT. Yes, I suppose so.

JANE. Unless, of course, home is no good either. Then there isn't much of a choice.

MATT. No. You're right.

JANE. So I'll stay.

MATT. Yes.

JANE. That's excellent advice.

MATT. Well.

JANE. Thanks for your help.

MATT. That's…that's what I'm here for.

Scene 6

(*In the kitchen.*)

ESTHER. My mother used to say that the secret to a great marriage was shift work. Decades and decades of shift work.

PHYL. My mother said it was frying onions. Have onions frying when he came in the door at night.

ALISON. Unbelievable.

PHYL. She had a cast iron frying pan that weighed more than she did.

ESTHER. Marriage is ridiculous. A waste of valuable time.

MARGE. So sentimental, our Esther.

PHYL. What about you, Alison?

ESTHER: Are you married?

(**ALISON** *doesn't respond*)

MARGE. You don't have to answer that.

PHYL. Kids?

MARGE. No need to answer that, either.

ESTHER. And what are you, Marge? Her lawyer?

ALISON: (*to* **PHYL**) Are you married?

PHYL. Well,....

ESTHER. Phyl's husband....

PHYL. Yes, I am married.

ESTHER. (*interrupting*) That's enough of that. Coffee time. It's a miracle we ever get any food done for these things.

MARGE. But we do.

ESTHER. Alison, there's a kettle behind you. Right there. You owe me a few favours, I'd say.

ALISON. I do not owe you favours.

ESTHER. Three favours, in fact. Or maybe three dozen. Come on. Help me with the coffee. After that you can go home.

ALISON. (*She grabs the kettle.*) This is such a sick way to spend a morning.

ESTHER. Alison?

ALISON. I'm coming.

ESTHER. Phyl, Marge, you two keep working. We're behind by my watch.

MARGE. We're always behind by your watch.

ESTHER. And I'm always right. We'll be back.

(*Exit* **ESTHER** *and* **ALISON**)

MARGE. (*sitting, tired*) God, she's a tyrant.

PHYL. Gosh. Would you like a sandwich, Marge?

MARGE. No. No sandwiches, thanks.

PHYL. What, are you done with sandwiches?

MARGE. Yes, I am. I am done with tiny sandwiches and I am bored to death with Jello salads.

PHYL. (*pause*) It's a gorgeous day out. I'll bet Ray's doing leaves today.

MARGE. He is.

PHYL. And when does Julie's gang arrive?

MARGE. Tomorrow.

PHYL. He'll be excited, then. (*pause*) Two caskets. That's a new one. Do you mind if *I* have a sandwich? I like the triangles. Maybe a chocolate-coconut square, too.

MARGE. Knock yourself out.

PHYL. (*pause*) Two caskets. Would she have her body in one and all her worldly possessions in the other, do you think?

MARGE. I can't stand the way we cut those squares into such small bits.

PHYL. Or maybe some parts of herself in one and some in the other.

MARGE. So small you can hardly taste them.

PHYL. I'd put my thin parts in one and my fat parts in the other.

MARGE. So small you can hardly breathe.

PHYL. Except for that plantar wart on my left foot. I'd give that a box of its own.

MARGE. And what is it with Jello? Someone gets sick again, and dies, and we break out the Jello mould.

PHYL. You know plantar warts, they last forever. They'll have to bury it alive. So that's three boxes for me.

MARGE. You know, we watch someone die and then we make Jello. And then, right away, someone else gets sick and dies and we make Jello again.

PHYL. Course, that third box would be a pretty small one, with just the wart. Those roots go way in, though. They'd take up a bit of room. (*pause*) Marge?

MARGE. What if making the Jello is what makes the next person get sick and die? Maybe then we should stop making Jello. We should stop cutting the crusts off the goddamned sandwiches.

PHYL. Three boxes.

MARGE. We should….

PHYL. Me, my fat, and my wart.

MARGE. I saw that bozo at the clinic on Thursday.

PHYL. Don't.

MARGE. I was supposed to go a year this time, but I've been tired.

PHYL. You need more naps. You don't take naps.

MARGE. It's funny. You're tired, and you can never know, anymore, whether it's back again or whether you just need to get to bed earlier.

PHYL. You need sleep. And you need to eat.

MARGE. I want to talk to you about something.

PHYL. That's what you need. A snack and a nap.

MARGE. In case it's more…

PHYL. (*cutting her off*) Be quiet.

MARGE. Phyl.

PHYL. No. You be quiet. You were fine last time, right? You've been swimming. You're fine.

MARGE. Phyl, I don't feel right.

PHYL. Stop it.

MARGE. Listen.

PHYL. No. I don't want to hear that. If you set your mind to it, you'll be all right. You told me that. I have to leave.

MARGE. For God's sake, Phyl.

PHYL. Do not bring God into this. I have to leave.

MARGE. Please stay.

PHYL. This is not hard. You're fine. I'll just go downtown, right now, and get the date squares, and we'll cut them up when I get back. We'll cut them up into smaller squares. Everything'll be fine. (*Exit* **PHYL**)

MARGE. Phyl?

Scene 7

(*In the bathroom.* **ALISON** *is filling the kettle*)

ESTHER. Fill it with cold, right up to the top. I'll make a cup for Matt. That's enough water.

ALISON. You said to the top.

ESTHER. That's close enough.

ALISON. You're not easy to get along with.

ESTHER. Well, thank God for you being Miss Congeniality, then. I'm wearing too much makeup.

ALISON. You got that right.

ESTHER. I knew it. It's ridiculous.

ALISON. Don't take it all off. Just do this with your fingers. Not like that. Don't rub. Blend. Like this. Here. I'll do it. (**ALISON** *changes* **ESTHER**'s *makeup.*)

ESTHER. I wanted to look like spring.

ALISON. You look like a crack-head.

ESTHER. Watch my eyes. Are your hands clean? The last thing I need is infected eyes.

ALISON. Like you don't look totally infected with all that makeup on. Stay still. Who's Matt?

ESTHER. Well, he's…. He owns this place. Can you lighten up a touch with your blending? I'm going to lose an eye.

ALISON. You might look better with one eye.

ESTHER. He was a cop here until last year. Not tough enough, but…. Anyway, the OPP moved in a few years ago and just took right over. And then, at a town council meeting two years ago, there was a vote, and they just let Matt go. The mayor, Phyl's fathead cousin-in-law-and-no-fault-of-Phyl's, said he was sorry, but they couldn't justify paying $38,000 for a friendly face, with the OPP only a phone call away.

ALISON. So.

ESTHER. (**ESTHER** *looks for cups, paper towels, etc., under the sink.*) So. With one bad vote and a majority *this big* (*she holds her finger and thumb up, indicating a narrow margin*), Matt's career was over. It was a stupid decision. So, we just scraped him off the floor – that took a bit of doing – and he took over here when Al Stinson retired in May.

ALISON. What do you mean it took a bit of doing?

ESTHER. Well how would you feel if you were fired, basically, by your own town council? So I help out here a bit with the Last Suppers.

ALISON. Why do you help?

ESTHER. Well, it's the decent thing to do. To help your neighbour.

ALISON. Is he your neighbour?

ESTHER. (*raising her voice*) No, I don't mean the neighbour that lives beside you.

ALISON. You mean the one that doesn't?

ESTHER. Yes. I mean the one that doesn't.

ALISON. You don't have yell. I can hear you.

ESTHER. You're so…. You bring three flowers. You think your neighbour is the person who lives beside you. He was never my neighbour.

ALISON. All right. Shit.

ESTHER. He was my husband.

ALISON. What?

ESTHER. You heard me.

ALISON. Shit.

ESTHER. My hair looks foolish.

ALISON. Wait. (**ALISON** *takes* **ESTHER**'s *hands, and does her hair.*) Don't touch it, you'll make it worse.

ESTHER. I don't know what happened. It started with small things. His pauses. The way he considered everything to death. He didn't boil an egg without thinking about it for an hour. I could see myself sitting at that kitchen table during those pauses, going nowhere together for another forty years and then dying, and not even knowing I was dead for a while, 'cause there wouldn't be any difference. Then all of it – the blue bows on the wallpaper in the kitchen – and I picked that wallpaper – the sound of the neighbour's Basset hound barking every time I turned the outside lights on – I just wanted to kick that dog in the head. I wanted to scream all the time. And one day it happened.

ALISON. You kicked the dog.

ESTHER. No, I didn't kick the dog! You don't kick dogs. I just blew, I told him I had to leave. His face looked so small. He has a small head, and it looked smaller than ever right then. I took a suitcase to this one-bedroom above the Mike's Mart on Stanley. Everything in that place, even the toaster, was greasy on your fingers. And the cigarette smoke….

Three days after I left, he called and asked would I like to go for coffee. I said I won't come back, and he said, I know, it's just coffee. So we met at the Tim's downtown. He was waiting at one of those tables for four in that corner by the bathrooms. With a coffee for me. Medium, just milk. Same thing the next day. We've had coffee almost every morning since. Six years.

ALISON. Really?

ESTHER. After a year or so, I asked him who in their right mind would ask me out three days after I'd done that? I mean, was he not hurt, or angry? And he said, oh, sure, he was all of that. But you can only be angry for so long, he said.

ALISON. No way.

ESTHER. How can a man like that survive without neighbours, without someone's help?

ALISON. (*reaching for the cups*) Gimme those.

ESTHER. So I know I'm difficult to get along with.

ALISON. I've met worse. Not many, but I've met worse.

Scene 8

(*In the chapel*)

(*Enter* ANNIE)

ANNIE: $4.50 for a litre of 2%, I can't believe it. Now that is whacked!

JANE. No one's going to come to this thing.

ANNIE. She's a closed box, Janie. In fact, of course, she's two closed boxes. I need a smoke.

JANE. No, you do not. Listen, Matt, the funeral guy, he wants stories for this…this not-funeral thing. Warm, funny stories.

ANNIE. You know, maybe Mom didn't make it to the warm phase of her life. Maybe if she'd lived into her eighties she'd have become funny. Not likely. Forgiving. Not likely.

JANE. He said we should look through her purse.

ANNIE. Jesus, is that her purse? She probably had her hands on that.

JANE. He said we'd like it because it's something personal.

ANNIE. Her fingerprints'll be all over it.

JANE. You know, she is multiplying. She's in three places, now.

ANNIE. On the other hand, maybe there'll be cash in there.

(ANNIE *takes the purse.*)

JANE. Don't touch it.

ANNIE. Or smokes. (*She reaches in*) Or Kleenex. Ooo, that's personal. (*finding a cell phone*) Hey.

JANE. A cell phone.

ANNIE. She must have lost my number. And yours.

JANE. Do you think her voice is in there somewhere?

ANNIE. That's creepy. Do you want it?

JANE. No.

(JANE *puts the phone in the bag*)

ANNIE. Look, it's a little key. Looks like a key to a diary. Or a very small heart.

JANE. What else?

ANNIE. Paper. Two sheets. They'll be notes saying, gosh, you two were the best.

JANE. (*taking the papers*) It's weird to see her writing.

ANNIE. Or receipts for two caskets and a funeral with no guests.

JANE: It might be private or something.

ANNIE. What do you think, Mom? Do you mind? Woop, still not talking to us. Go ahead.

JANE. (*She puts her glasses on.*) Coffee cream. Two Ida Reds.

ANNIE. When did you get the glasses?

JANE. Last year.

ANNIE. You look like her.

JANE. No, I don't. Toothpaste.

ANNIE. Tough to get a really personal picture of her life from toothpaste.

JANE. Then library.

ANNIE. Library what?

JANE. It just says library.

ANNIE. Hey. Here's a lipstick. Same colour as always. Looks just like yours.

JANE. Does not.

ANNIE. Look, it's the same colour.

JANE. Mine isn't as dark.

ANNIE. Maybe you're losing your colour vision, too.

JANE. Or maybe you're demented. This is a totally different colour.

ANNIE. Okay, stink bomb.

JANE. Bloodsucker fish. Do you remember anything about her?

ANNIE. I remember that winter coat, you know, the black

one, from the....

JANE. The one with the hood and the hairy arms....

ANNIE. Yeah, and she'd do it up and she'd look just like that, you know that song....

(**ANNIE** *begins to laugh*)

(*To the tune of Itsy Bitsy Spider,* **JANE** *sings Extremely Small Tarantula Climbed Up The Bedroom Wall.* **JANE** *is deadly serious throughout the singing.* **ANNIE** *joins in, less seriously.*)

JANE. And she'd pull on her hood to flatten the....

ANNIE. But she looked even worse then.

JANE. Which made you laugh.

ANNIE. Which made her mad.

JANE. She hated kids' songs. Why would you hate kids' songs?

ANNIE. Who cares? It was four million years ago.

JANE. I loved that song.

ANNIE. So that's good, right? Is that the kind of story your funeral director is looking for?

JANE. You're a jerk.

ANNIE. Of course I am. And you're a snotlicker. Give me the other paper.

(**JANE** *passes the second note to* **ANNIE**.)

JANE. What.

ANNIE. Daisies. Three of them. Look. I love daisies. What's that beside them?

JANE. (*taking the paper*) I hate flowers.

ANNIE. You do not.

JANE. They stink. October third. October tenth.

(**JANE** *freezes.*)

ANNIE. (*taking the paper back*) October seventeenth. One daisy for each. That's just last week, the seventeenth. Which day?

JANE. I don't know. Who cares?

ANNIE: It was Sunday.

JANE. It might be some other year, for all we know. Jeez, you know, I left my, I left something in the car.

(**JANE** *gets up to leave*)

ANNIE. Last Sunday, the seventeenth. That was the day I quit. So they're all Sundays, right? The third, the tenth, the seventeenth.

JANE. I don't know, and so what, anyway? It doesn't tell us anything.

ANNIE. Maybe she was going to church. Not likely.

JANE. Let's get a coffee. Or lunch. Or dinner.

(**JANE** *grabs the note back and crumples it.*)

ANNIE. Wait. Don't throw it out. You were the one who mentioned the purse, for Christ's sake.

JANE. Take it, then.

(**JANE** *throws it back at* **ANNIE**)

ANNIE. And why daisies, do you think? Maybe she knew she'd be pushing them up soon.

JANE. You are disgusting.

ANNIE. She used to call Gran on Sundays, remember? They'd yack for an hour, the two of them. Sundays at ten. She said it was better than church.

JANE. (*stopping in her tracks*) What?

ANNIE. I don't know what that'd have to do with daisies, though. Mom said it took her a year after Gran died to stop picking up the phone on Sundays.

JANE. I don't remember that.

ANNIE. Will it take *us* years to stop calling? Woop, guess we're over *that* part, already, aren't we Mum?

JANE. Be quiet.

ANNIE. Quiet yourself. If she'd called me once in the last ten years, I'd keep my voice down.

JANE. Please, just shut up. She's right there.

ANNIE. All right, all right. Something warm, all right.

JANE. Just shut up!

ANNIE. Responsible sister has nervous breakdown at mother's funeral. Younger sister, jerk, apologizes.

JANE. Shut up!

ANNIE. It's okay, Janie. It's okay.

Scene 9

(*At the lectern*)

(*Enter* **DELIVERY #6**)

DELIVERY #6. Carmichael.

MATT. Thank you. That looks great. If you'll just….

ESTHER. That way. Turn left. (*Exit* **DELIVERY #6**) Carmichael looks huge.

MATT. Bigger than we thought, but it seems to be running well.

ESTHER. It's hard to keep food hot as the numbers go up.

MATT. Helen seems to think it'll be all right. (*He sees* **ESTHER***'s reaction*) Course what does she know? No. Have you seen any flowers for Bain?

ESTHER. Not yet.

MATT. How are things in the back?

ESTHER. Tip top. We're almost ready to go. It was nothing. I could have done both. Easily.

MATT. Well. I'll get back to the front, then. I'll be with the Carmichaels if anyone needs me.

ESTHER. I won't need you. Everything is fine back there.

MATT. You look different today, Esther. Did you do something with your hair?

ESTHER. No, just the same old thing. You know, Matt, I've been thinking of cutting back on dutchies. They can't be good for you. Do you even like dutchies?

MATT. I do. I like them.

ESTHER. But those crullers, they're terrible. That saturated fat, you know,....

MATT. I like the crullers.

ESTHER. Well, that's good. And they taste good, I know, I just thought....

MATT. Of course, if *you* want to cut back....

ESTHER. No, I don't want to cut back, I just meant.... I was thinking of something different.

MATT. We can go every other day, if you like.

ESTHER. No, no.

MATT. Or every third day.

ESTHER. No. I love the crullers. I eat them at home, sometimes, you know, while I'm at home. Sometimes I eat two. And then a dutchie. I was just thinking about... arteries and things.

MATT. Arteries?

ESTHER. Yes, and cholesterol. Bad habits.

MATT. You think it's a bad habit?

ESTHER. No, not the dutchies. Not Tim's. I don't mean that. It's more about the arteries.

MATT. I haven't thought much about arteries. What about arteries?

ESTHER. It's nothing. It's not about that. Forget I said anything. We've got work to do.

MATT. Yes, we do, I suppose, but if you....

ESTHER. Right.

MATT. I'd be happy to hear about your arteries.

ESTHER. Oh, never mind.

   (*Exit* **ESTHER**)

MATT. What did I say?

   (*Exit* **MATT**)

Scene 10

(*In the kitchen*)

ALISON. I'm gonna leave now. This is kind of a loser way to spend the day, putting out sandwiches for dead people.

MARGE. You're right.

ALISON. Got a busy day ahead. No offence.

MARGE. None taken.

ALISON. But, you know, I did tell Esther I'd stay. Make the porridge. Apparently she wants the porridge, yeah. How strange is that? Shit. I'll stay for a couple of minutes. This sucks.

(*Enter* **ESTHER**)

ESTHER. Well, things are looking great in here. And our timing is perfect. Everybody happy? Marge?

(*Enter* **PHYL**. *She is a wreck.*)

PHYL. I have date squares.

ESTHER. Phyl, you are a saint.

PHYL. I have cream of wheat.

ESTHER. Oh, for God's sake.

PHYL. No hearts. So I got stars.

ALISON. I'll take those.

ESTHER. Phyl, why are you helping Marge make ridiculous food?

PHYL. Do you think they had enough time with us?

ESTHER. What? Who?

PHYL. The ones who died. Bronwyn Bain. I can't help wondering. About whether she had enough time to say everything she wanted to say. About whether she finally had all the books she wanted. About whether she can actually rest in peace. I didn't have enough time with my mom. How could you ever have enough time? For the last few years she didn't even know us, my brother and me. She thought I was her sister, Gracie. She thought I was poisoning her food. We'd go to the Manor, my brother and I, I'd bring a banana loaf or some brownies, which she wouldn't eat. He'd pull out his guitar and we'd sing, (*singing*) "All of me" – it was her favourite song – "Why not take all of me". And this huge smile would crack her face open, and she'd limp along with us: (*singing*) "Can't see…no good…out… you". There wasn't a person in that room who could carry a tune. Tone deaf, every one of us.

ESTHER. Phyl? (**PHYL** *doesn't answer*) My mom loved the Lone Ranger song.

(*All but* **PHYL** *sing it, all keeping an eye on* **PHYL**.)

ESTHER. I think she had a thing for him. A good, reliable guy on a horse. You know. She hummed it, too, whenever she didn't want to hear what we were telling her. You'd say, Mom, I think it's time you gave up driving. After that time she wiped out the mail boxes by her place. And she'd start humming. (She hums a bit)

MARGE. My mom's was *Softly and Tenderly*. (*She sings a few bars.* **ESTHER** *joins in*) "Softly and tenderly Jesus is calling. Calling all sinners come home". It was her dad's favourite song. That was my Gump. He'd cry when you sang that to him – after his stroke, anyway. He was an awful man before the stroke, but he softened up after.

PHYL. He was not awful.

MARGE. (*angrily*) Yes he was, Phyl. Anyway, after his stroke, I'd say don't cry, Gump. You can't afford to lose the weight. Cause he'd lost so much weight, then. After, when we carried him out of the church, it was as though we were carrying air, he was so light. How does someone disappear like that?

ALISON. My mom doesn't sing.

ESTHER. That can't be right. Everyone sings. Even Phyl sings in the car. I sound great in the car. I sound like Ella Fitzgerald.

ALISON. (*angrily*) I said she doesn't sing. She never sings.

What's wrong with that?

ESTHER. Nothing wrong with that. No. That's good. That's fine. OK, then. Phyl, bring me the date squares. I think we're going to be all right this afternoon.

PHYL. You know, there's this man who hangs around in periodicals at the library, he's this huge hulking troll of a man. He looks like something from under a bridge in a fairy tale.

MARGE. Phyl, if this is another story about mahogany caskets and bursting with grief, I'm going to scream.

PHYL. His hair just pours down, black as black, from the top of his head down to his elbows. No one goes near him. He reads this small paperback – he brings it with him to the library – why would you do that? – and it looks really small because his hands are so big, each finger is like a sausage. He stands, facing the window in periodicals, and just reads his paperback. I try to get closer, sometimes, to see the title, but I swear there's a kind of invisible wall around him. All I can think of when I see him is that there is no way I breastfed my son long enough. Every time Aiden has a cold, and he's 26 for God's sake, I'm positive it's because I didn't breastfeed him long enough. Someone should have breastfed that man longer. Someone should still be breastfeeding that man. I could be this Bain woman. Buried in pieces. (*pause*) I miss being kissed.

MARGE. I love being kissed.

PHYL. You don't deserve to be kissed.

MARGE. Oh, yes I do.

ESTHER. (*quietly, almost to herself*) I miss being kissed. (*Seeing the others' reactions*) What's wrong with that?

PHYL. If I could be anything today, I'd be kissed.

MARGE: I'd be kissed in the water. In the deep end, kissing my Ray.

PHYL. If I could be anything, I'd be Franklin the Turtle.

ALISON. Franklin the Turtle?

ESTHER. It's a long story. Don't get her started. I'd be a

nun.

PHYL. You would not!

ESTHER. Really, I would be. Married to God.

MARGE. With his hands on my face, and the sound of his voice right here.

PHYL. We do not need to hear about his hands on your face, Marge. What is the point of hearing that? And you (*to* **ESTHER**), how can you even joke about being a nun, with all your profanity, tossing off God and Jesus Murphy and the rest like they were crumbs off a bad loaf of bread.

ESTHER. Well, why not? If you can be Franklin, why can't I be a nun? And if God is the Great Organizer – and he would be, wouldn't he, Phyl? – then I'd be married to someone just like me. That'd be great. We'd run the town. And God's got everything figured out, already, right? So I wouldn't have to wait for him to think. He'd know the difference between heart disease and lunch, for God's sake. There'd be no having to get your words right. With men, you know, it's so much…. I think you have an effect on the man you're with, and maybe it isn't always good. And I wonder, if I was "married to God", well, maybe God could handle me without being adversely affected. If you know what I mean.

PHYL. If I could pick two things, I'd be Franklin the Turtle on the first day and a real nun, married to God, on the second. Can we pick two? I'm picking two. I want to be a nun who was a nun right from the start, though. No Jim.

MARGE. Phyl, you don't mean that. You loved Jim. Don't leave him out.

PHYL. Don't you tell me who to leave out or what it is I mean. You tell me one thing.

ESTHER. OK, Alison, now you tell me who's sounding a little tense now? A little overdressed, whatever that means.

PHYL. Did you not say that you could make yourself healthy?

And I thought you were crazy. But here you are. And you're fine. So you were right and I was wrong.

MARGE. Phyl….

PHYL. So just stop with all that business before, about wanting to talk to me about anything else.

MARGE. I think it's back.

PHYL. Don't say that.

MARGE. Please listen to me.

PHYL. Do not say that. And don't tell me I can't be a nun who never knew my Jim.

ESTHER. Phyl….

PHYL. If you can throw everything away, so can I.

MARGE. I'm not throwing anything away.

ESTHER. Phyl, Marge. Come on, now. Both of you stop it.

MARGE. You…you are as stubborn as Jim was.

PHYL. Don't you mention Jim.

MARGE. He was a stubborn man.

PHYL. You have no right to say anything about him….

MARGE. He was stubborn and he was hard on Aiden from the time that boy learned to walk.

ESTHER. Marge, what are you….

PHYL. What are you doing?

MARGE. He wasn't perfect.

PHYL. Why are you saying this….

MARGE. He drank too much.

PHYL. No. Stop.

ESTHER. Marge.

PHYL. You're being cruel!

MARGE. He drank till he couldn't see straight, some nights with Ray.

PHYL. I'm leaving. I can't do this.

MARGE. Don't leave. Stay. I'm trying to tell you something.

PHYL. I don't want to hear what you're saying.

MARGE. Please stay.

PHYL. I will not stay. How dare you talk about my husband like that? You are horrible. Do you hear me? You ass…bag…head. (*She throws food.*) You are an awful human being!

MARGE. Yes, I am.

ESTHER. Marge! Phyl!

MARGE. (*throwing food.*) I am awful!

(**PHYL** *and* **MARGE** *continue to throw food during the following lines.*)

ESTHER. Pull yourselves together!

PHYL. How dare you!

MARGE. Listen to me!

ESTHER. Stop it, for God's sake! Please, you two!

PHYL. How dare you say these….

MARGE. I am awful!

ESTHER. Stop shouting! You're making a mess of everything!

PHYL. You, you're,…you….

MARGE. We're all awful, aren't we?! I'm cruel, you're right, and you're stuck. You're so stuck, you haven't changed your clothes since Jim died.

PHYL. Don't!

MARGE. And Esther, well…. And what happens to all of that? We get sick and die or we get hit by a bus and die, who knows, and all of a sudden people are eating Jello salads with coconut – who came up with dessicated coconut, I'd like to know – and going on about how we were so selfless and kind and perfect, till you could choke on it! We do it here every week, we make these goddamned sandwiches with white bread on one side and brown on the other, with pink cream cheese in the middle– what the hell is that all about? We do it to our friends and our mothers and our husbands. I don't want the crusts cut off when I'm dead! Can you hear me?! I want it all there. Good, bad, and ugly. Three caskets. Breastfeed *that*! Inject *that* into your veins! Radiate yourself with it. For God's sake, Phyl, do you not miss the awful things about Jim?

PHYL. I loved my husband. He was a saint. And I've had more than I can take of you. If this is friendship, these things you're saying, I don't want it! (*She turns to leave.*)

MARGE. You know what, Phyl? The last thing I need today is the sight of your self-righteous fat ass stomping away in front of me. And if you don't want this friendship, I can certainly do without.

(*Exit* MARGE)

PHYL. I can't believe this! I can't believe it!

(*Exit* PHYL)

(ESTHER *and* ALISON *survey the mess*)

ESTHER. You cannot just blow up and leave. You can't just create disasters wherever you go. Are you listening to me? You can't!

(*Exit* ESTHER)

ALISON. I'm sorry.

(*Enter* ESTHER)

ESTHER. The day is ruined, isn't it! Look at this. Matt is going to.... And of course Helen'll just sweep in and.... And those two! Do you see what they've done to each other? Can they not hear each other, for Christ's sake? You can't just blow up and leave! (*Exit* ESTHER)

ALISON. I'm sorry.

(*Curtain*)

ACT TWO

Scene 1

(*In the chapel*)

(*Enter* **MATT**, *with a remote and a lamp, which he plugs in.*)

MATT. Well, Anne. You're back.

ANNIE. I am.

MATT. There. Look. (*He clicks the remote, and the pictures, with heads missing, begin to flash.*) I think they look just fine, don't you?

ANNIE. They're certainly…big.

MATT. Yes, well. They say that if you live a large life, your ending won't be so…

ANNIE. So what? So small?

MATT. I'm sorry, I've got that wrong.

ANNIE. Can we help you with something, Matt?

MATT. Yes, well, I was wondering whether you'd like any help with the retrospective. Your stories.

ANNIE. They're just pouring out of us now.

MATT. Good. That's wonderful. And I'm sure you won't be the only ones sharing.

ANNIE. Why, do you have stories?

MATT. About your mother?

ANNIE. Right.

MATT. Well, no. I didn't know her at all, except for our one meeting here, but her friends, your friends,…. Well, I suppose we'll just do what we can. Why don't I check on the flowers.

JANE. Do you not think that flowers are completely pointless?

MATT. Well, if you need me at all, just call.

(*Exit* **MATT**)

JANE. Annie, we haven't seen each other in two years.

ANNIE. People drift. I've been busy.

JANE. You live four blocks away.

ANNIE. It's five blocks.

JANE. Four and a half. (*pause*) I miss you.

ANNIE. I've been busy. Mixing paint. Painting.

JANE. And you hate it.

ANNIE. I hate mixing. Not painting.

(*pause*)

JANE. You mean painting painting?

ANNIE: Yes, I mean painting. Janie, do not say anything. Please, for the love of God, do not say anything except "good for you", 'cause if you do, if you say anything shitty, I'll leave this second and I will never forgive you. Say "good for you, Annie".

(**JANE** *nods.*)

ANNIE. Say it.

JANE. Good for you, Annie.

ANNIE. Peter is an interview.

JANE. What do you mean, Peter is an interview?

ANNIE. It's nothing.

JANE. It doesn't sound like nothing.

ANNIE. He has a gallery. He saw something he liked on an old website.

JANE. Which one?

ANNIE. Downtown Iris.

JANE. That woman.

ANNIE. Yeah.

JANE. On Queen Street.

ANNIE. Just say, "good for you, Annie".

JANE. That was good.

ANNIE. So I'm taking him some new stuff, just to show him.

JANE. New stuff?

ANNIE. It stinks, maybe, and it's been, like, seven thousand years since I've....

JANE. Good for you, Annie.

ANNIE. Jesus, and I was shitty even when I was good, I don't know what I'm doing.

JANE. Annie. Good for you.

ANNIE. I don't want any calls from you saying how'd it go. Just leave it, all right?

JANE. All right.

ANNIE. I'll stay for the purse. Then I gotta go.

JANE. I don't want to do the purse.

ANNIE. Chicken liver.

JANE. I hate being here. I hate all of this.

ANNIE: Two sisters, one middle-aged and miserable, one much younger, much more fun to be with, brought together, at last, by hating all of this.

(*Enter* **MATT**, *with another lamp. During this scene he plugs it in and turns it on.*)

MATT. Excuse me. I said before that I didn't know your mother.

JANE. Yeah.

MATT. That I only spoke with her that once when she came in to make final arrangements.

JANE. Yeah.

MATT. That's all true.

ANNIE. It's good of you to confirm that, Matt.

MATT. Yes.

ANNIE. Sometimes it's good to hear things more than once.

MATT. So I didn't really know her friends. But maybe you do. Know some friends we might call for this afternoon. Because I'm not having much luck in that direction.

JANE. Oh.

ANNIE. Well.

JANE. We should tell you something.

(*Enter* **ESTHER**. *She's a mess, covered with flour, curls not what they were.*)

ESTHER. Excuse me.

MATT. Esther.

ESTHER. I'm sorry to interrupt. The kitchen is…. We were making sandwiches and…. I had it completely organized. Everything is going to be…. Would you like a coffee? It's not hot, but it's…. it's cold. I could make more.

MATT. I'd love one.

ESTHER. Here. It's cold.

MATT. I like it cold.

ESTHER. I'll bring you another one later, a hot one.

MATT. Are you all right, Esther?

ESTHER. Tip. Top. Everything is just fine. Excuse me.

(*Exit* **ESTHER**)

MATT. Esther and I are…. We've known each other for 21 years. On Wednesday, it'll be 21 years. I don't think she would care to hear that. Her hair looks different today. She's a very interesting woman. Just this morning, she mentioned arteries, which is a completely new area of interest, as far as I know.

It could be that she's also interested in capillaries. There's a lot to think about, there, with blood vessels.

(*Exit* **MATT**)

ANNIE. Far too young for me, but I like him. Come on, let's finish the purse. (*She picks up the purse*)

JANE. (*Reaches for the purse*) I'm going to say it one more time. I don't want to do the purse. Can you hear that? It's brutal, touching her things. It's none of our business.

ANNIE. Janie. (*She grabs the purse back and begins to look through it.*) Lighten up, will you, for once in your life. I'm trying to do the right thing. It's the first time in twenty years, don't get in my way.

JANE. Leave it.

ANNIE. Jane, back off, will you? Christ, is it any wonder we don't get together, ever? Stop telling me what I should do, what I shouldn't do. I'm doing the purse. End of story. (*pause*) You know, maybe the daisies on the paper meant something. Loves me, loves me not, and all of that.

JANE. Enough with the daisies, will you? They're irrelevant, Annie. You're such a...you're unbelievable.

ANNIE. I know what I am, thanks very much. Okay, forget it. No more daisies. You were the one who showed me the purse. The daisies, woops, forget I said that, were in the purse. Take it easy.

JANE. Don't tell me to take it easy.

ANNIE. Look. Tweezers. Or will tweezers piss you off, too? They're good ones, too. Do you want them? I'll take them.

JANE. (*upset*) Why? Why would she carry tweezers in her purse?

ANNIE. Maybe she liked plucking her eyebrows while she was out shopping.

JANE. Tweezers, Jesus.

ANNIE. Some eyeliner. I've got a kind of Joan Crawford thing going in my head, now.

JANE. Oh, that's nice.

ANNIE. (*bringing a small case from the purse.*) Some kind of case. Locked.

JANE. Just as well.

ANNIE. The whole purse should be locked. Hey. I'll bet that's what that little key's for. Where's the key?

JANE. I don't know.

ANNIE. (*finds the key*) Look, it fits.

JANE. What is it?

ANNIE. It's a picture, and confetti or something.

JANE. What are these little bits?

ANNIE. (*looking at the picture*) It's us. Look.

JANE. You and me?

ANNIE. And her.

JANE. I don't remember that.

ANNIE. It's your first communion. I remember the crown thing.

JANE. (*remembering*) She made those dresses.

ANNIE. Yours is blue.

JANE. And yours is purple. Why did you always get purple?

ANNIE. I dunno. Cause you always got blue. They had that matching embroidery or something across the front.

JANE. Look at her. She's smiling. God. She looks so happy.

ANNIE. It's weird, seeing her happy. They were flowers, weren't they, across the front?

JANE. Yeah.

ANNIE. It must have taken her forever to do those. These daisies, do you think....

JANE. Leave them. Leave them alone.

ANNIE. Do you think there's any chance – you know, do you think there's any chance she thought about us in the last while, before she died?

JANE. No. I don't. She didn't.

ANNIE. How do you know that? I could be wrong. Maybe I've been wrong. How can we....

JANE. Stop it, Annie.

ANNIE. Show me the other stuff.

JANE. No.

ANNIE. I want to see it.

JANE. I don't want to.

ANNIE. Come on, Janie. Show me the bits. What are they?

JANE. Don't.

ANNIE. What?

JANE. Leave it!

ANNIE. Show me.

JANE. This is sick.

(ANNIE *grabs the bits.*)

ANNIE. What is it?

JANE. No.

ANNIE. Oh my God.

JANE. I have to go.

ANNIE. It's Dad's heads.

JANE. Don't say that.

ANNIE. Dad's heads. I'm sure that's him. It is. It's Dad. He looks good.

JANE. Jesus!

ANNIE. Hey, Dad.

JANE. We ought to be in an institution of some kind, don't you think? For looking at any of this. For coming here at all.

ANNIE. What do you mean?

JANE. Can we not just bury her, Annie? She left. She went away, she stayed away. End of story. Didn't write, didn't call, didn't return calls. What do you want? I don't know if she was cracked in the head or just didn't care. At all. So the key here, the little key here, is just to put her away somewhere, completely, every piece of her, in the ground, and get the hell out of here. Gone. Over. Done with. Dad's heads, Annie? God, she must have been crazy.

ANNIE. I don't think so.

JANE. I need to go.

ANNIE. Maybe she just left and couldn't come back.

JANE. I've got to go. I'm sorry.

ANNIE. Maybe she just left and then she couldn't figure out how to make it better.

JANE. I'll see you later.

ANNIE. Do you not wish you could fix any of this?

JANE. No, I can't fix it. I tried and tried and tried.

ANNIE. What if we could? You know what? I *am* a jerk. You're right, and I'm a coward, and yes, I wish that I could...that I could love a man for more than six weeks at a time. I wish that we could see each other without it blowing up every time. I wish you were nicer to be with, and you know what, Janie? You're not. I wish I'd had the basic courage to stop mixing paint five minutes after I had the job. I mixed paint for seven years, for Christ's sake. Jesus. I could end up in there, I know it. A couple of pathetic pizza boxes in an empty funeral home. Can't do that, Janie. I have to try something else. And what if I'm wrong about her, what if I've been wrong? Tell me. Tell me, for fuck's sake. (**JANE** *doesn't respond*) Jesus.

(*Exit* **ANNIE** *to the bathroom.*)

(*Enter* **MATT**)

MATT. How are you doing with the purse?

JANE: It's a great purse. Lots of compartments. It's strange to think that when we were leaving messages, she was off to the library and the grocery store. For Ida Reds. Getting her lipstick right, plucking her eyebrows. And just not returning calls. For years.

Then there's gravity. These boxes'll just get heavier and heavier. And they'll multiply. There'll be seven or eight of them before you know it and she will never be gone.

(**JANE** *laughs*) Maybe I'm cracked. (*To* **MATT**) Nice day outside. Not many crimes being committed. (*To herself*) Not many.

Scene 2

(*In the bathroom.* **PHYL** *is a mess, covered in food fight debris.*)

(**ALISON** *is nearby – close enough to hear the conversation*)

ANNIE. Wrong fucking door. I need a smoke.

PHYL. Oh, that's lovely language.

ANNIE. Go to hell.

PHYL. You go to hell.

ANNIE. And my hair is a disaster. Do you have a cigarette?

PHYL. You go to hell.

ANNIE: Thank you for your generosity.

PHYL. You'll die of cancer smoking those.

ANNIE. Why is my hair such a disaster?

PHYL. It's the humidity. That's October for you.

ANNIE. It was October yesterday, and my hair was fine.

PHYL. Maybe you're wrong. Maybe your hair was a disaster yesterday, too.

ANNIE. You're a sick woman.

PHYL. Yes I am. Have you got any clips, or bobby pins?

ANNIE. Do I look like I have hair clips?

PHYL. (*taking* **ANNIE***'s hair*) Here, hold still. I'll try not to get too close. Wouldn't want you catching anything.

ANNIE. Some hairdresser.

PHYL. I thought of being a hairdresser once.

ANNIE. Me, too. Then I wanted to be a marine biologist. Everyone wants to be a marine biologist at one point. I need a cigarette so badly.

PHYL. Two years ago, I was Franklin the Turtle.

ANNIE. I do not care about that.

PHYL. The library held a children's day during the March Break, and 53 children showed up to meet Franklin. But the costume that arrived on the bus from Ottawa that morning didn't fit Sylvia, my supervisor, who was supposed to be Franklin. And that costume has to fit just right or you can't see out of Franklin's mouth. (*To* **ANNIE**) Give me your finger. (*She uses* **ANNIE**'s *finger to hold some hair in place*) So, with no notice whatsoever, I had to be Franklin.

You should have seen the kids' faces. It was the way they looked at me. Or at Franklin. I mean, I know they weren't looking at me, but they looked...they made me feel as though I had never once in my life made a mistake. Can you imagine that?

ANNIE. Never making a mistake?

PHYL: No. I mean having someone look at you as though you've never made a mistake. When they looked at me like that, I felt safe.

ANNIE. Who are you?

PHYL. I was safe for six months. I'm Phyllis. I'm a librarian. No, that's wrong. I *was* a librarian. You know, people come, and go. You can't seem to count on anything. They fire you, or not fire you, exactly, but let you go, which is worse....

ANNIE. Bastards.

PHYL. They are bastards. It's a horrible word, but it's true. They get sick and they die, don't they? They die, without giving you a chance to have any real time with them....

ANNIE. Bastards.

PHYL. So you do everything you can to stay away from it all, but you can't leave it, can you?

ANNIE. Oh, sure you can.

PHYL. No you can't. You can try, and it might feel like it's working for a while, but you can't just be married to God. Were you ever a nun?

ANNIE. No.

PHYL. You know, if I could be anything today, I'd be looking out my kitchen window, with everything all right. But I can't do that.

ANNIE. But you *can* leave. We can leave. I'm leaving.

PHYL. No you can't leave. You know why? Because if you leave the part that you can't stand, the part that shoots through you like some kind of bursting aneurysm myocardial stroke thing – if you leave that part, you're leaving Jim altogether.

ANNIE. Well I can leave Jim, whoever Jim is. I can leave anyone.

PHYL. No you can't. It'll be fifteen months on Wednesday. You can't leave these awful numbers – fifteen months, his birthday coming up on the twenty-ninth, we would have been married twenty-eight years, he died eleven days after his cough was looked at. (*pause*) They called it a galloping cancer, like it was something at a bastard fall fair. You know, he came home after that first appointment with the specialist and he was sitting in the car, in the driveway, for I don't know how long. I could see him out the kitchen window. I was making potato salad, a new one, with an oil dressing, instead of mayonnaise. Black olives. When he pulled in, I was peeling the potatoes. I should have known. I watched him while they boiled, and then while they cooled, and he didn't look up once to see me. I kept chopping and chopping the olives, waiting for him. They were in the smallest pieces by the time I finally made myself go out there. He kept his hands on the wheel while he told me. Both hands on the wheel. And then, right away, he got out of the car, and put up the hood, and showed me how to check the oil. He laughed, watching me do it. I was so mad at him. I thought, he should be taking this seriously, shouldn't he? But you know, who am I to say how we should be? How we should do it. Who am I to say for the others?

ANNIE. What others?

PHYL. Marge. The Last Supper Committee. We were in the other room, making food for the funeral this afternoon.

ANNIE. It's not a funeral.

PHYL. What's the difference?

ANNIE. I dunno.

PHYL. Are you the daughter?

ANNIE. One of them.

PHYL. And you're leaving?

(**ANNIE** *nods.*)

PHYL. For good?

(**ANNIE** *nods*)

PHYL. You have to stay.

ANNIE. I'd be completely cracked to stay. You wouldn't understand.

PHYL. I don't have to understand. You have to stay.

ANNIE. You just said you can't tell the others how to do it.

PHYL. You're right, you're absolutely right. Do what you want, then, be your own marine biologist.

ANNIE. I tried to stay. I did, but I keep making mistakes.

PHYL. That doesn't matter.

ANNIE. Yes, it does.

PHYL. No it doesn't. Think of Franklin. What matters is looking at each other as though we've never made mistakes. That's what matters. Give me your other hand (She puts it in place, holding some hair). You shouldn't chew those nails. And you know, if you stopped smoking, you wouldn't be so nervous to begin with.

Scene 3

(*In the chapel.*)

JANE. I have a story.

MATT. That's good to hear. It'll make you feel better.

JANE. I'm tired. I need some air.

(*pause*)

MATT. That's a good story.

JANE. (*to the casket*) Are you listening? This would have been a lot easier if you'd written a letter, instead.

Scene 4

(**ESTHER**, *and* **MATT**, *with coffee, at the lectern.* **ESTHER** *is stunned.*)

(*Enter* **DELIVERY PERSON #7**)

DELIVERY #7. Carmichael.

(**MATT** *stares at him/her for a moment, but says nothing*)

ESTHER. That way.

(*Exit* **DELIVERY #7**)

ESTHER. Carmichael.

MATT. You have something on your blouse.

ESTHER. Oh.

MATT. And in your hair. There.

ESTHER. It's nothing.

MATT. And here. Smells like salmon.

ESTHER. Thanks.

MATT. Did you have a good morning back there?

ESTHER. Not tip top.

MATT. Esther? Have any flower arrangements come through the kitchen?

ESTHER. Well, no.

MATT. How is the food looking?

ESTHER. It could be better.

MATT. Esther, did any of your friends in the kitchen know Mrs. Bain?

ESTHER. Not really.

MATT. I wonder if the Last Supper Women might stay for the visitation. Just in case we need to fill the place up a bit.

ESTHER. They've all.... There was this.... I don't know if there's anyone left. Well, in fact, I do know. There's no one left. Unless Alison stayed, but she didn't want to be here in the first place, so she'll be gone, too. I've made a mess.... Are there any guests, yet?

MATT. No.

ESTHER. Just the daughter?

MATT. There were two daughters. They may have gone.

ESTHER. Well, this just can't be. We'll have to get moving, find some more people, some more sandwiches. Marge and Phyl are.... There's no time...and the food is all over.... I don't know what to do.

MATT. Esther? Thanks for the coffee.

ESTHER. The coffee, Matt? The coffee? There's no time for that. You should see the kitchen. Coffee, for God's sake!

MATT. It's all I can do. I've written a three-line obituary, I called about the flowers – I don't know what's going on, there. And I don't know if anyone is coming this afternoon.

ESTHER. So think of something else.

MATT. I've done everything I know how, Esther. The one good thing I can think of, now, is to thank you for the coffee.

ESTHER. When everything is gone to hell. Blown to smithereens.

MATT. Yes.

ESTHER. When people have said horrible things.

MATT. Yes.

ESTHER. And nothing can possibly work out.

MATT. One good thing.

ESTHER. Thank you for coffee.

MATT. Yes.

(*pause*)

ESTHER. Matt? Would you like to try coffee with lunch tomorrow?

MATT: At Tim's?

ESTHER. Or dinner. At my place.

MATT. That's a kind offer. I'd like to think about it, if you don't mind.

ESTHER. Fair enough. It was a thought that crossed my mind. Just now. It doesn't matter one way or another. I just thought I'm a bit tired of dutchies. And muffins.

MATT. Is it the arteries?

ESTHER. Not really, no.

MATT. I'd like to think about it.

ESTHER. And Timbits. I'm tired of Timbits.

(**MATT** *nods his head.*)

(*pause*)

ESTHER: Okay, then. Thank you for thinking about it.

(*Exit* **ESTHER**)

MATT. Okay, then.

(*Enter* **ALISON**, *with her coat on*)

MATT. Are you with Carmichael?

ALISON. I brought flowers for Bain.

MATT. Good. How many arrangements?

(*pause*)

ALISON: Three.

MATT. Well, that's a start.

ALISON. Have you ever met someone who didn't get any flowers when she died?

MATT. Well….

ALISON. What if someone was such a total loser that no one showed up for the funeral? What would you do then? Would you just leave her here and go home?

MATT. No. I'd stay.

ALISON. Even if you were the only one?

MATT. Yes.

ALISON. Bullshit, and you didn't even know her?

MATT. Yes.

ALISON. Why? Why would you stay?

MATT. Because you have to help, where you can, with the family, if there is one, and their stories,…

ALISON. What if there are only bad stories?

MATT. There's no such thing as only bad stories. Stories are made up. So you tell the good stories.

ALISON. So, you just make them up?

MATT. I don't know what you do. We had a funeral here last week. A man showed up and told a story about the deceased taking his driver's exam. There was something about opening the sunroof every time it started to rain. (**MATT** *laughs*) And the driver's ed guy getting soaked. Turned out this guy telling the story, he had the wrong funeral altogether. Came to Thursday's funeral on Friday. But it was good to laugh. So I just know that good stories are better. Did you know Mrs. Bain?

ALISON. Only what I heard this morning, in the kitchen. Was she alone when she died?

(*pause*)

MATT. Yes, she was. It was a stroke. A neighbour found her a few days later. There were fliers were piling up at the front door.

ALISON. She has a kid here?

MATT. I hope so. Will you stay?

ALISON: I've been trying to leave all morning.

MATT. Bit like her dying all over again if no one's here for her. I suppose they cooked up a storm back there this morning.

ALISON. You could say that, yeah.

MATT. Thank you for the flowers.

(*pause*)

ALISON. We should thank Esther, I think.

MATT. I will.

ALISON. We hit it off right from the start. She's great.

MATT. Yes, she is.

ALISON. She's pretty hot, don't you think?

MATT. I haven't thought about that. For a long time.

ALISON. Maybe you should. I gotta go.

(*Exit* **ALISON**)

Scene 5

(**MARGE** *sits on a bench, in the back alley. She is covered with flour.*)

(*Enter* **ESTHER**)

ESTHER. I need your help.

MARGE. It's been a long day, Esther. I don't need company.

ESTHER. Fine, then. You want to throw away a perfectly fine friendship, you go to it. But Matt asked me to do this event, and that's what I'm going to do. The Bain visitation is spread all over the place in there.

MARGE. She is completely obsessed with all of this, with heart attacks and strokes and aneurysms, and broken tiles the size of loonies. And her clothes, for God's sake, she's like a vulture. Doesn't it feel like she's flying in circles over your head? I can't stand it.

ESTHER. Jim died with about three minutes notice – of course she's different. She's bleak and black and she's taken ownership of Jesus, all of a sudden, that's the way it is. But you don't say those things to her face, for God's sake. And to say those things about Jim…. I don't know what the hell you were doing.

MARGE. Well, what the hell is she doing, turning these people into saints? Into something so perfect that they couldn't have been here at all? I hate that. Can't you see what's happening?

ESTHER. You don't want to be sick again, that's what I see happening. You don't want to join Mrs. Bain or Susan or Jim or your mother or my mother. No one wants to join that line-up.

MARGE. That isn't what I'm saying.

ESTHER. So while you're figuring out what it is that you do want to say, stop being mean to Phyl. She doesn't need it. She'll come out of it soon enough. Throw some food at me, if it'll make you feel better.

MARGE. Oh, for God's sake. I hate this food.

ESTHER. It's your food, Marge, smell it. Here, throw some salmon. (*She picks something off her sweater/out of her hair.*) Throw some cilantro, Marge. It's just a garnish. Come on. Where are the eggs? Where are they?

MARGE. I'll crack one over your head.

ESTHER. Crack two. Come on.

(**ESTHER** *takes* **MARGE** *by the arm and pulls her toward the kitchen.*)

MARGE. Esther…

ESTHER. What do you want? Jalapenos? Is that what you want?

MARGE. Yes, I want jalapenos. That's exactly what I want. (*pause*) Thank you for asking. What do you want?

ESTHER. I want,…I want lunch. Lunch or dinner. Either one. I'm flexible.

MARGE. Esther?
ESTHER. What?
MARGE. You're so flexible it hurts.

Scene 6

(**ALISON** *enters the chapel with the three flowers and her scissors. She looks around the room, and leaves.*)

Scene 7

(**PHYL** *is in the kitchen, sitting. Enter* **MARGE**)

PHYL. I forgot my purse.

MARGE. I'm sorry.

PHYL. I didn't think it would happen. Even while it was happening, I thought, this isn't happening. But it was.

MARGE. It was awful. I....

PHYL. At three, she handed me my purse. She handed it to me, and just stood there until I left the library. I don't even know if I can borrow books anymore. Do you know what they said to me?

MARGE. What did they say?

PHYL. It won't go on my official record, as if that matters, but they said they'd lost confidence in me, in my ability to do the right thing. They said someone had to put a stop to it.

MARGE. I'm sorry, Phyl. And I'm sorry about what I said.

PHYL. Don't.

MARGE. I wasn't trying to be cruel. I was trying to tell you something....

PHYL. Do not tell me anything. Please.

MARGE. All right. Will you try this?

(**MARGE** *hands* **PHYL** *a colourful scarf.*)

PHYL. I don't like it.

MARGE. For five minutes.

PHYL. It's too much.

MARGE. Just put it in your pocket. For two minutes.

PHYL. I'll look like an over-the-hill skateboarder, with no helmet. I'll crack my head open, my brains'll spill out. There'll be no one to help,....

MARGE. Phyl, it's a scarf. It's a bit of colour.

PHYL. People should be more careful with colour. They have no idea what can happen. (*pause*) You're never afraid.

MARGE. Of course I'm afraid. Do you think I'm a dimwit? Some days I can hardly breathe.

PHYL. I wish I could help.

MARGE. You can.

PHYL. I said I wish. It wasn't an offer.

MARGE. I want to teach you how to swim.

PHYL. Swimmers die in the water, Marge. One big gulp and it's all over.

MARGE. Everybody dies, Phyl. Me, you. (*Enter* **ESTHER**) Everybody dies. You should learn to float before you die.

PHYL. I don't want to die in the water.

ESTHER. Oh, for God's sake.

MARGE. Please, Phyl.

PHYL. I'll think about it.

ESTHER. Don't mind me. I'll just sweep up around you while you plan your death by drowning, you two.

(**ESTHER** *begins to sweep.*)

(*Enter* **ALISON**)

ALISON. I was fired this morning. So basically, I can't go home today. It's too hard on my mom. (*She begins to leave, and comes back.*) I try to do good things, but they get turned around. So now I'm just trying to keep my mouth shut. (*She begins to leave, and comes back.*) I'm also pregnant, which isn't good. (*pause*) There's no guy. Well, there was sperm, you know how it is, but.... I was so stupid. You know, this Mrs. Bain, she's doing all right. If someone took me, right now, and put me in some boxes, piece by piece, I wouldn't take up much room, you know, which would be good, and I'd stop breathing, after a while, which would kinda be a relief, at this point. What do you think?

ESTHER. Well, Alison,....

(*Exit* **ALISON** *to chapel*)

ESTHER. Marge! Phyl! Help out, for Christ's sake. Speak up.

MARGE. Poor kid.

PHYL. Holy Mackerel.

ESTHER. We have to do something.

(*Enter* **ALISON**)

ALISON. I don't know my mother's favourite song. Maybe if she was dead I'd know it. My brother's dead, though. He was skiing at Lake Louise. Anyway, he was killed in an avalanche, day after Christmas. I have this dream, sometimes, and in it, I was with him, holding his hand while it happened. So he wouldn't be alone. Maybe it would have been more like going to sleep, then. I could say, shhhh, and he could just close his eyes. Twinkle Twinkle Little Star. Billy's song. Maybe it wasn't his favourite, but it was the one he sang with me. (*She sings a few lines of a rap version, with actions*)

(*pause*)

ESTHER. That's a fantastic song. (*pause*) Isn't that a fantastic song?

PHYL. I thought it was more of a children's song.

ALISON. No it isn't.

ESTHER: Cripes.

MARGE. Alison. Sing it again. We'll do it with you.

PHYL. I can't sing.

MARGE. Yes you can. You can sing.

ALISON. Up above the world so high....

> (*They sing a few lines, imitating* **ALISON**'s *rap singing and actions.* **ALISON** *struggles toward the end, and they trail off.*)

MARGE. It'll be all right, Alison.

ALISON. You can't say that. How do you know?

ESTHER. Because I'm older. I'm smarter. Well, maybe not smarter. I'm more organized.

ALISON. That's bullshit.

ESTHER. You're right. I don't mean that.

MARGE. We'll stay here until it is all right.

ALISON. How? What can *you* do?

PHYL. We'll do our best, which is what we're all doing, all the time.

MARGE: Look at me. We'll do our best.

ESTHER. See? See? That's right. That's what I meant. We'll do our best. Jesus, God, this is going to kill me, this job.

Scene 8

(*In the chapel*)

(*Enter* **MATT**, *who sits, looking at the new flowers made by* **ALISON**.)

(*Enter* **ANNIE**)

ANNIE. Hey. (*seeing the flowers*) Wow.

MATT. Hey.

ANNIE. Have I missed it? The funeral thing, the....?

MATT. Celebration of Life. You haven't missed it.

ANNIE. Where's Janie?

MATT. I don't know.

ANNIE. Did she leave?

MATT. I hope not.

ANNIE. I hope not, too, her being the only child and all. (**MATT** *looks uncomfortable.*) Just messing with you, Matt.

(*Enter* **JANE.**)

ANNIE. Hey.

JANE. You stayed.

ANNIE. Thank that hairdresser in the bathroom.

JANE. I shouldn't have come.

ANNIE. We could make a run for it right now if you want, Janie.

MATT. Well, then. I'll tell the others we're almost ready.

ANNIE. There are others?

MATT. There's Esther.

(*Exit* **MATT**)

JANE. I have to tell you something.

ANNIE. What's that?

JANE. It's something bad.

ANNIE. You know what, Janie? Whatever it is, let's just say, "Good for you", ok? Can we just forget all the bad stuff, for now, and just say, "Good for you"? Can we do that?

JANE. I have to tell you.

(*Enter the women from the kitchen, and* **MATT**. *The women have plates of poorly reassembled food, and a bowl of punch.* **MATT** *uses a remote to turn on the headless pictures, which provide a continuous slide show during the service. The Last Supper Women see the pictures for the first time during* **MATT**'s *welcome.*)

MATT. Here we are. Welcome, everyone. Welcome to Mrs. Bronwyn Bain's farewell. We're a little late starting, but I wanted to make sure we could all make it. This is good. We have chosen to bid her farewell by sharing our thoughts and memories together. To tell a story or two over a glass of punch. Feel free to enjoy sandwiches and...(*he notices the mess assembled on the plates*) a few other snacks while we chat. Who would like to start? (*The women have passed the plates around*) Jane, Annie, when you've had a bite, I wonder whether you'd begin by sharing with us some of the memories you discussed this morning.

ANNIE. Oh my God this is hot! Oh, God. Oh, shit. Is there water?

PHYL: Have some punch.

MARGE. It's jalapeno pie.

ESTHER. I knew it was too hot.

ANNIE. It's fantastic!

PHYL. Try a bit of porridge.

ANNIE. Oh, my God!

PHYL. It'll cool your mouth.

ESTHER. Or a square. There are squares. Have two.

PHYL. Have three.

ESTHER. Have two.

PHYL. (*to* **MARGE**) She's a marine biologist.

ANNIE. It's so hot!

MARGE. Jalapenos. They're fantastic for you.

ESTHER. Would you like a little sandwich? Have some ham.

ANNIE. Thank you.

PHYL. There are carrots. And ranch dip. Here.

JANE. No. Thanks.

ESTHER. No crusts on those sandwiches. (*They all drink, and eat. A prolonged silence.*)

MATT. Jane? Annie?

(*pause*)

JANE. I don't know what to say. I don't have any.... My mother....

(*pause*)

ESTHER: (*desperately*) Your mother was a great snacker. Yes,

I remember how much she loved that trail mix with the dried cranberries in it. She had excellent taste. In snacks. (*pause*) And Phyl, you knew her from the library, didn't you?

PHYL. Yes. Your mother loved books.

ANNIE: She did love books.

PHYL. She collected books.

JANE. I didn't know that.

PHYL. Yes, she did. We had a kind of relationship at the library.

ALISON/MARGE. Perhaps.

ANNIE. Perhaps what?

PHYL. Perhaps we have all kinds of stories about your mother. She had a carport, of course, which is unusual in the north. (*No one speaks.*) In fact, she had a bit of an interest in carports.

JANE. What do you mean? Do you mean architecturally?

PHYL. Yes, architecturally…and in other ways.

JANE. What ways?

PHYL. Well,…environmentally. (*pause*) They only have two walls, you know, so they use fewer…. walls.

ANNIE. I think I can picture that.

JANE. Did no one know her?

ANNIE. Sure they knew her. They're telling us they knew her. Aren't you?

(*pause*)

MARGE: Your mother wasn't an easy woman.

ANNIE. No, she wasn't.

MARGE. She made people uncomfortable. She wasn't friendly.

ESTHER. Marge.

JANE. You're right. She wasn't friendly.

MARGE. She alienated people at the checkout when she got her groceries.

ANNIE. See, they did know her.

MARGE. Let me tell you about what she did at the library.

ESTHER. Marge? Marge, don't tell all the stories. Let the rest of us have a chance.

ANNIE. I'd like to hear more.

(*pause*)

MARGE. She used to go to the library, without her books, and….

ESTHER. Marge. Let…let someone else get a word in.

(*Another silence*)

ALISON. I knew her.

ESTHER. What?

ALISON. I knew her.

PHYL/MARGE/ESTHER/MATT. You did?/What?

ALISON. A little bit, yeah. I was with her when she died.

ALL. You were?/What?

ALISON. Yes. I was on one of my morning walks, with Aiden, my son – he had a cold. I don't think I breastfed him long enough. Anyway, I was taking him for a walk and I saw her place, on Ferguson. The one with the carport. There were fliers piled up in the mailbox, and some underneath, on the front step. I thought I'd pick them up. Then I heard the radio, so I knocked a couple of times, and tried the front door. It was open, so I said hello. She answered, your mom, from her bedroom. She was sitting up with pillows propped behind her, reading a paperback. I didn't look close enough to see the title. She said she'd been too tired to clean up the mail for a few days. I made us some tea.

ANNIE. She did drink tea.

ALISON. And we talked. She showed me lots of pictures, from scrapbooks she'd made. Some of you two, as kids. One of her, floating in a pool.

JANE. We never had a pool.

ALISON. Maybe it was from a vacation. I don't remember.

She said she loved floating in the deep end. And then there was a funny one of her in a turtle costume.

JANE. A turtle costume?

ANNIE. What is it with these turtles?

PHYL. How do you know about her turtle costume?

ESTHER. Mrs. Bain's turtle costume?

ALISON. She also said how much her friends meant to her. And she could be unfriendly at times, but her friends were there for her. She said the Last Supper Committee changed her life. (*to* **JANE** *and* **ANNIE**) And she wished she'd been able to see her kids again.

ANNIE. That's incredible.

ESTHER. Absolutely incredible.

ALISON. And then we sang a few songs with Aiden, and drank our tea. Earl Grey tea, I think it was.

JANE. Earl Grey.

ALISON. We had some shortbread.

ANNIE. She loved shortbread.

ALISON. It was imported. Looked expensive.

ESTHER. She loved that shortbread.

ALISON. Then I put Aiden on the bed, and I took her cup to the kitchen. When I came back, her eyes were closed, and her hands were resting on the pictures on her lap. She hadn't even taken her glasses off.

ANNIE. We saw her glasses today.

PHYL. She died then?

ALISON. Just as peaceful as that. She just went to sleep. I held her hand for a while, and then I called Mr. Watson.

JANE. So.

ANNIE. Wow.

MATT. Well.

ANNIE. I'm glad you were there. All of you.

ESTHER. Well. Us, too.

PHYL. What are friends for?

(*pause*)

ESTHER. Alison, what songs did Mrs. Bain sing with Aiden?

ALISON. What?

ESTHER. You mentioned singing songs with Aiden.

ALISON. Right. All of Me. Why not take all of me.

PHYL. I love that song.

JANE. It's a strange choice for Mum.

ALISON. Maybe we didn't sing that one. Maybe it was playing when we got there. But we sang that Lone Ranger song.

JANE. 1812 Overture.

ANNIE. She'd love that.

ALISON. Softly and Tenderly. It's a hymn, I think.

MARGE. It is. It's a hymn.

ALISON. And Twinkle Twinkle Little Star.

JANE. Twinkle Twinkle? I don't think so.

PHYL. (*to* **MARGE** *or* **ESTHER**, *in order to distract* **JANE** *and* **ANNIE**) I think she may have taken a book out on The Lone Ranger.

ANNIE. She wasn't into kids' songs.

ALISON. (*angrily*) It is not a kids' song. And she sang it all the time. With her friends. (*She begins to sing it, and the Last Supper women join in.*)

(*pause*)

ANNIE. That is great.

(*pause*)

JANE. (*cracking up, slightly*) It's a beautiful song. Thank you. For the flowers, which are…, and your stories. I don't know how much you, I mean if you really knew….

(*Pause*)

MATT. So, if that's all, from everyone, perhaps we'll gather up our….

ANNIE. Wait. I have a story. About my mother. If we have time. My sister Jane and I were going through some picture bits. My mother made us these dresses when Jane had her first communion. I was seven, I think. The other girls all wore white dresses. That's what you did, for first communion. But our dresses were blue and purple. We looked like crayons in a bag of marshmallows. We were gorgeous. And all over them she embroidered white daisies with green leaves. She did it by hand. She loved her daisies. In the picture, she looked really happy with us. I have it, if you'd like to see it. She probably wouldn't mind me showing it to her friends.

MATT. We'd love to see it.

MARGE. I'd love to see her.

PHYL. Me, too.

ESTHER. Me, too. Eat up, please. We have all this food. Have a sandwich, Marge.

MARGE. Is there any porridge left?

PHYL. I love these squares.

(**ALISON** *passes trays of food, humming*)

(*Exit* **MATT**, *exit* **ALISON** *and* **ESTHER** *to the bathroom,* **MARGE** *and* **PHYL** *to the kitchen*)

Scene 9

(**ESTHER** *and* **ALISON** *in the bathroom*)

ESTHER. Did you rehearse all of that, or does it just come out all by itself? (*Exit* **ESTHER** *to kitchen*)

(**MARGE** *and* **PHYL**, *in the kitchen*)

PHYL. Just so I'm clear about this, Alison wasn't actually with Bronwyn when she died.

MARGE. No, Phyl. She wasn't.

PHYL. It sounded real.

MARGE. Architectural interest in carports? That was good, Phyl.

PHYL. I'm doing my best, Marge.

MARGE. Whatever it takes, Phyl.

(*Exit* **PHYL**)

Scene 10

(**JANE** *and* **ANNIE**, *in the chapel*)

ANNIE. God, it's hard to believe, with the turtle and everything, but she had so much right: the glasses, the tea, the unpleasant part. And I can picture it, Mum changing a bit, given enough time. I mean, look at her carrying that picture in her purse. And Dad's heads. Maybe she was warming up.

JANE. Thanks for coming, Annie.

ANNIE. Do you think she was telling the truth, that woman? Do you think Mom said all that stuff?

JANE. Yes I do. (*She's lying.*)

ANNIE. Do you have time for a coffee, Janie? Or 2%? Or a 40 of vodka?

God, my mouth is still burning.

JANE. You won't be late for your meeting with the guy?

ANNIE. No. I'll be there. You know, I was hoping we might go over a few things for the interview. I'm looking for a way to make seven years of mixing paint sound like a success story.

JANE. It'll be all right.

ANNIE. Thanks, Janie. For all of it.

JANE. I'll meet you outside in a minute, OK?

ANNIE. You all right?

(*Enter* **MATT**, *who begins to clean up.*)

JANE. Yeah. (**ANNIE** *begins to leave.*) Annie?

ANNIE. Yeah?

JANE. I don't think they knew her.

ANNIE. Yes, they did.

JANE. I don't think they knew her. I don't think she had friends.

ANNIE. Please don't say that.

JANE. Your story about the dresses was great.

ANNIE. I think they probably knew her.

JANE. I have another daisy story.

ANNIE. I'm pretty sure they were right.

JANE. October third was a Sunday. I was having a bad day, which is not that unusual anymore. I don't know why and I don't know what's happened to my life but, you know, who cares. The point is that on October third I was having a bad day. So I just didn't answer the phone when it rang. I didn't pick it up. And there was no message. On October tenth, which was also a Sunday, it rang again. At ten. I don't know how you know, but it rang four or five times and I thought, pick it up. It's her. Pick it up. And there was no message. But I knew. Last Sunday, I left the house at 9:30, just to be sure I wouldn't be there, because I had a feeling. And there was a message this time, but it was nothing. Just a few seconds of nothing, and then someone hanging up. That was October seventeenth. Three daisies.

ANNIE. Janie.

JANE. So there's my story.

(*Exit* **JANE** *to the back hallway of the funeral hall*)

MATT. Are you all right?

ANNIE. No, I'm not. All this time, she's…. She talks about why I should be here, and the whole time, she's…No, I'm not all right.

(*Exit* **ANNIE.** *She goes to the bathroom, and sits/stands in front of the mirror.*)

Scene 11

(*In the kitchen*)

MARGE. (*to* **ALISON**) Thank you for your…memories of Mrs. Bain, in there.

ESTHER. Not that yours weren't completely heart-warming, Marge, but I think Alison's timing was good. You know, before you got into the petty theft part of Mrs. Bain's life.

MARGE. I'd like to ask you three a favour. When my time comes, I'd like you to make my Last Supper. I want big sandwiches, Esther. Any filling you want, but I want the crusts left on.

ESTHER. Marge, not to make a point of it, but every time they take one of those sandwiches, they're taking four of the triangles. Four each. We could feed them asparagus and goat cheese for that kind of money.

MARGE. I want the sandwiches.

ESTHER. Marge….

MARGE. Phyl, you can make your squares.

PHYL. You don't like my squares.

MARGE. I've changed my mind. You can make whatever you like, for as long as you need to.

PHYL. Have you changed your mind about the swimming lessons?

MARGE. No, I have not. Will you let me teach you?

PHYL. It's pretty risky.

MARGE. I'd also like jalapeno pie. You start with an ovenproof dish. A layer of sliced, pickled jalapenos. You can get them at the ValuMart but they're cheaper in the huge jars at Costco, Esther. Half a big brick of old cheese grated over the jalapenos. Five eggs whisked and poured over top. Bake it at 325 for 50 minutes. Let it cool for a bit before you cut it.

ESTHER. People'll drop like flies, eating it.

PHYL. It'll burn holes in their throats.

ESTHER. It'll be great business for Matt.

MARGE. And about my service. I don't want, "she was kind".

PHYL. You were not always kind.

ESTHER. You were stubborn.

PHYL. You were too colourful. It was dangerous.

ESTHER. You were no good with authority. You never stuck to the schedule.

PHYL. You were too ready to give up on your friends.

ESTHER. You should have told your friends when their hair and makeup made them look like crack addicts.

ALISON. You were kind to strangers.

ESTHER. What?

ALISON. She was.

ESTHER. Marge doesn't want good things. She wants bad stories and three caskets.

ALISON. You can't just have bad stories. That'd be pathetic. I'm not cooking for it unless we have both.

PHYL. (*to* **MARGE**) I hope it's a long way off, your death.

ALISON. It'll be years.

ESTHER. How do you know? Oh, let me guess, because you're going to be by her side with tea when she goes, right?

MARGE. (*to* **PHYL**) I hope so, too.

PHYL. We'll do your lunch. If we're still here, cause you never know what might happen. I may drown before you go. Esther may be killed by one of those skateboarders.

ALISON. We'll do your lunch.

MARGE. Thank you.

Scene 12

(*In the back hallway*)

JANE. This is so stupid. (*into the cellphone*) Mum? Hi. I miss your.... I'm sorry for all the time we missed, and I'm sorry I didn't pick up when you called.

Scene 13

(*In the chapel, with* **MATT**, *and* **ESTHER**, *who's just come in from the kitchen*)

MATT. That was quite a funeral.

MATT/ESTHER. Not-funeral.

MATT. Thank you for bringing the Last Supper women.

ESTHER. It was nothing. It was no Carmichael.

MATT. I don't think Carmichael could possibly be this good. (*pause*) I didn't see the salmon.

ESTHER. It didn't make it out here. There might be a bit left in the back.

MATT. I'd love some.

ESTHER. I'll get you a plate.

MATT. I mean tomorrow, with coffee.

ESTHER. Where?

MATT. At your apartment. If you want to, still. I thought we might talk about blood vessels. And other things.

ESTHER. Well, I....

MATT. Just lunch, if you don't mind. They say you shouldn't drink coffee after lunch. I don't know whether that's a cholesterol thing, or an arterial thing, or something else altogether.

ESTHER. Good. That's good.

(*Exit* **ESTHER** *to the kitchen. Exit* **MATT**)

Scene 14

(*In the kitchen, with* **MARGE**, **PHYL**, *and* **ALISON** *cleaning up. They're humming. Enter* **ESTHER**.)

ALISON. I don't have a job.

ESTHER. Neither does Phyl, and she's all right.

PHYL. I'm all right.

ALISON. I'm really good with flowers, but not so good with the people part.

ESTHER. Aaahh, you're all right.

ALISON. (*to* **PHYL**, *after a pause*) I thought you and I could open a flower shop together. Both out of work, and me with a kid to take care of.

PHYL. I don't know.

MARGE. Phyl.

ESTHER. Phyl likes flowers.

PHYL. I also like books, but I'm not opening a library.

MARGE. You could use a bit of colour.

ALISON. I'm good at it. I really am.

MARGE. (*to* **PHYL**) You could work the counter.

ALISON. You'd take good care of people. I know you would.

PHYL. I like the people.

ALISON. So will you think about it? Please?

PHYL. Yes, I will.

ALISON. Thank you.

ESTHER. Jesus, Mary, and Joseph. Incredible.

MARGE. I knew it'd be a good day.

Scene 15

(*In the chapel*)

(*Enter* **JANE**. *She collects six flowers, puts three flowers on one casket.*)

(*Enter* **ANNIE**)

ANNIE. She looks good with flowers in her hair.

JANE. That's her hip.

ANNIE. That's okay.

JANE. No, it's not.

ANNIE. Look at me.

JANE. I should have picked up the phone.

ANNIE. No mistakes, Janie. It's a Franklin thing, a turtle thing, I'll tell you about it later. It's okay.

(*They put three more flowers on the other casket.*)

ANNIE. She's probably all excited after the Celebration.

JANE. Do you think she can hear us?

ANNIE. I don't know why not. Hey, ma, what's up? What's that? Oh, Janie's okay, don't worry, just a little messed up after the funeral. Oh, you're right, after the Celebration of Life. You *were* listening.

JANE. (*stiffly, and without enthusiasm*) Hi Mom.

ANNIE. (*to the casket*) Hey, those were good stories, today. You have some good friends, Mom. Yes you do. What's that? Some 2%? Sure, we happen to have some out in the car, don't we, Janie? Hey, Mom, tell her to brighten up, will you?

JANE. I'm trying. I am. (*She tries to smile. It looks ridiculous.*)

ANNIE. Come on, Mom, I'll help you up. (S*he picks up the boxes and they begin their exit*) Look at you twirling! That's pretty good, what with the hip and all.

JANE. Wait. Wait a second. I think we should leave her hip here.

ANNIE. That's kinda gross, Janie.

JANE. I think we got that multiplying…gravity thing all wrong. I don't think she wants the titanium anymore.

ANNIE. But she wanted both, she said she did.

JANE. People change. You said that.

ANNIE. Yes I did. (*She puts down one box.*) Okay. If that's what you want, both of you, I'm good with it. What do you think, Mom? Yeah? Hey. Good for you, Mom. Janie, say good for you. (*pause*) You said you would. Say good for you.

JANE. Good for you.

ANNIE. Now say good for us, Janie. Just say it.

JANE. (*unsure of herself*) Good for us.

ANNIE. Not bad, for your first try. It'll do. (*She lifts the one remaining box higher*)

(*During the following lines,* **JANE** *and* **ANNIE** *begin their exit. Their conversation fades*)

ANNIE. Mom, slow down, for God's sake, we can't keep up. Oh, she'll be all right, she's a little choked up, that's all. You could have choked on some of that food, I'll tell you, I don't know what they were doing with that. Maybe we'll hit the party up front for some decent food. Hey! Maybe they'd like the hip, too! There's an idea.

JANE. Stop. That's awful.

ANNIE. Why? I'll bet they've only got one measly casket up there so far. Big, honkin' funeral and only one casket, what's that about? It was a good day, wasn't it, Janie? It was. It was, it was a good day.

(*Closes with the Last Supper Women singing in the kitchen,* **MATT** *at the front desk,* **ANNIE** *and* **JANE** *leaving the chapel.*)

PROP LIST

Sunshine Chapel

7 Flower Arrangements

Many tissue paper flowers

2 small, cardboard file boxes with fitted lids, one box smaller than the other.

Small, low table for the boxes

3 lamps

1 remote control

7 chairs

vases

Take-out coffee cup

Purse, with cell phone, tissues, 2 sheets note paper, lipstick, eyeliner, tweezers, photograph, small bits of photographs, small key to fit small jewellery box, a pair of Glasses.

Slides of photographs

Bathroom

Vanity with small mirror

Stool

Coffee cups

Bobby pins

Kitchen

White board or large pad of paper

Markers

Clipboard with menu

2 work tables

Counter surface

Sink

Hot plate

Cutting boards

Wax paper

Aluminum foil

Doilies

Aprons on hooks

Punch bowl

Punch glasses

napkins

Stools

Scissors

Knives

Kettle

Tissue paper

Paper flowers

Pipe cleaners

Dishcloths

Broom

Folding tables

Trays

Flour

Colourful scarf for Marge

Jalapeno Pie

Salmon Souffle

Cilantro

Punch

4 Grocery Boxes/Bags (2 for Phyl)

Aprons

Sandwiches in plastic containers

Date squares

Various squares

Cream of wheat

Back Alley

Bench

Matt's Office/Reception Area

Telephone table

Chair

SET DESIGN

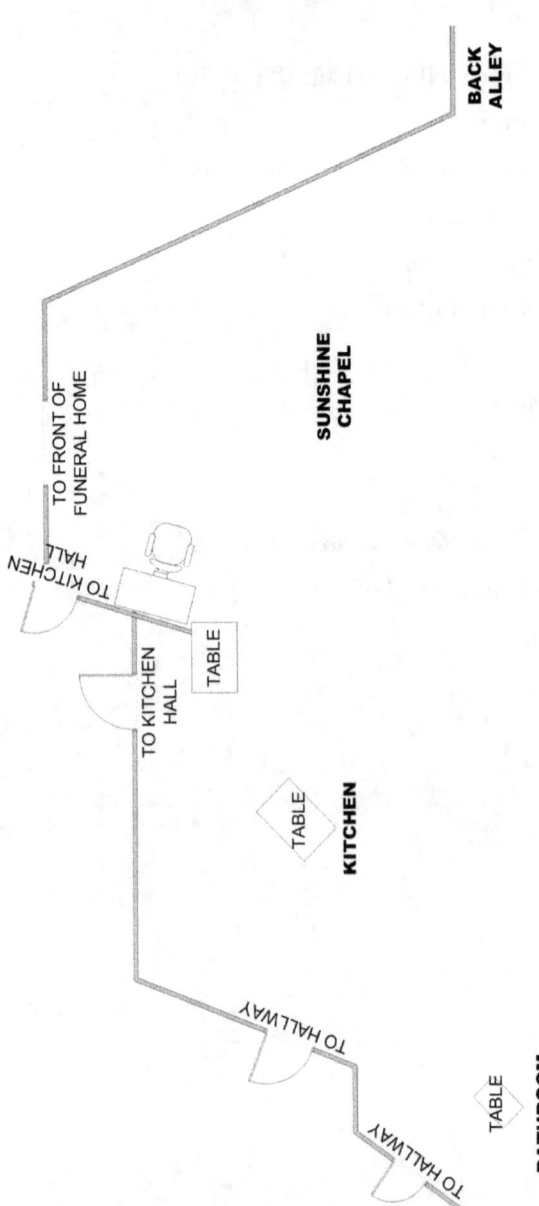

www.ingramcontent.com/pod-product-compliance
Lightning Source LLC
Chambersburg PA
CBHW070645300426
44111CB00013B/2280